# EUGENE SPRINGFIELD

*A Contemporary Portrait*

*The Eugene Area Chamber of Commerce and Community Communications, Inc. would like to thank the following companies for their leadership in the development of this book:*

EUGENE AIRPORT

Sony Disc Manufacturing

SPENCER VIEW DENTAL PARK

Valley River Inn
A WESTCOAST HOTEL

SPONSORED BY THE EUGENE AREA CHAMBER OF COMMERCE

PHOTOS BY BRUCE BERG

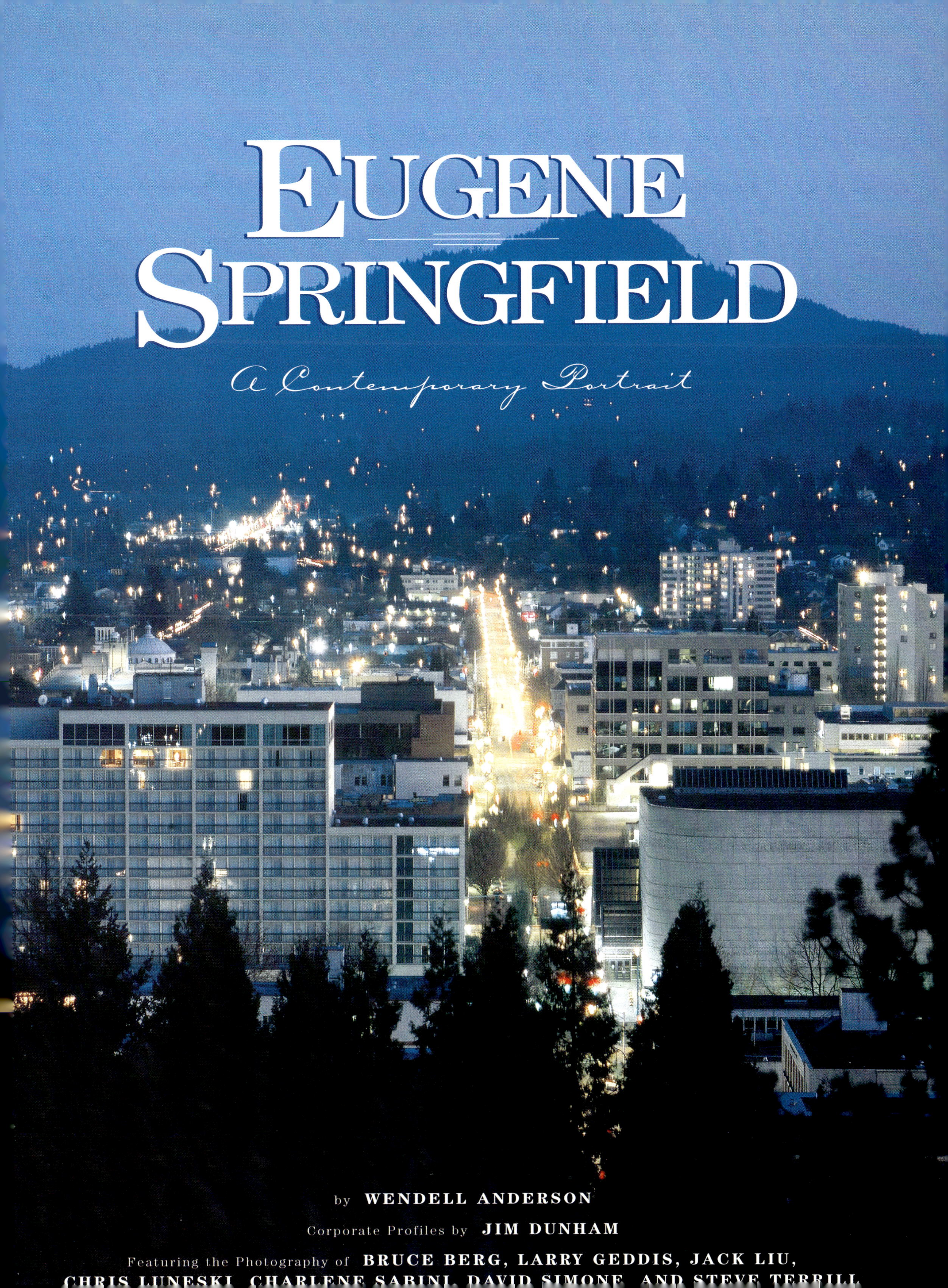

# EUGENE SPRINGFIELD

*A Contemporary Portrait*

by **WENDELL ANDERSON**

Corporate Profiles by **JIM DUNHAM**

Featuring the Photography of **BRUCE BERG, LARRY GEDDIS, JACK LIU, CHRIS LUNESKI, CHARLENE SABINI, DAVID SIMONE, AND STEVE TERRILL**

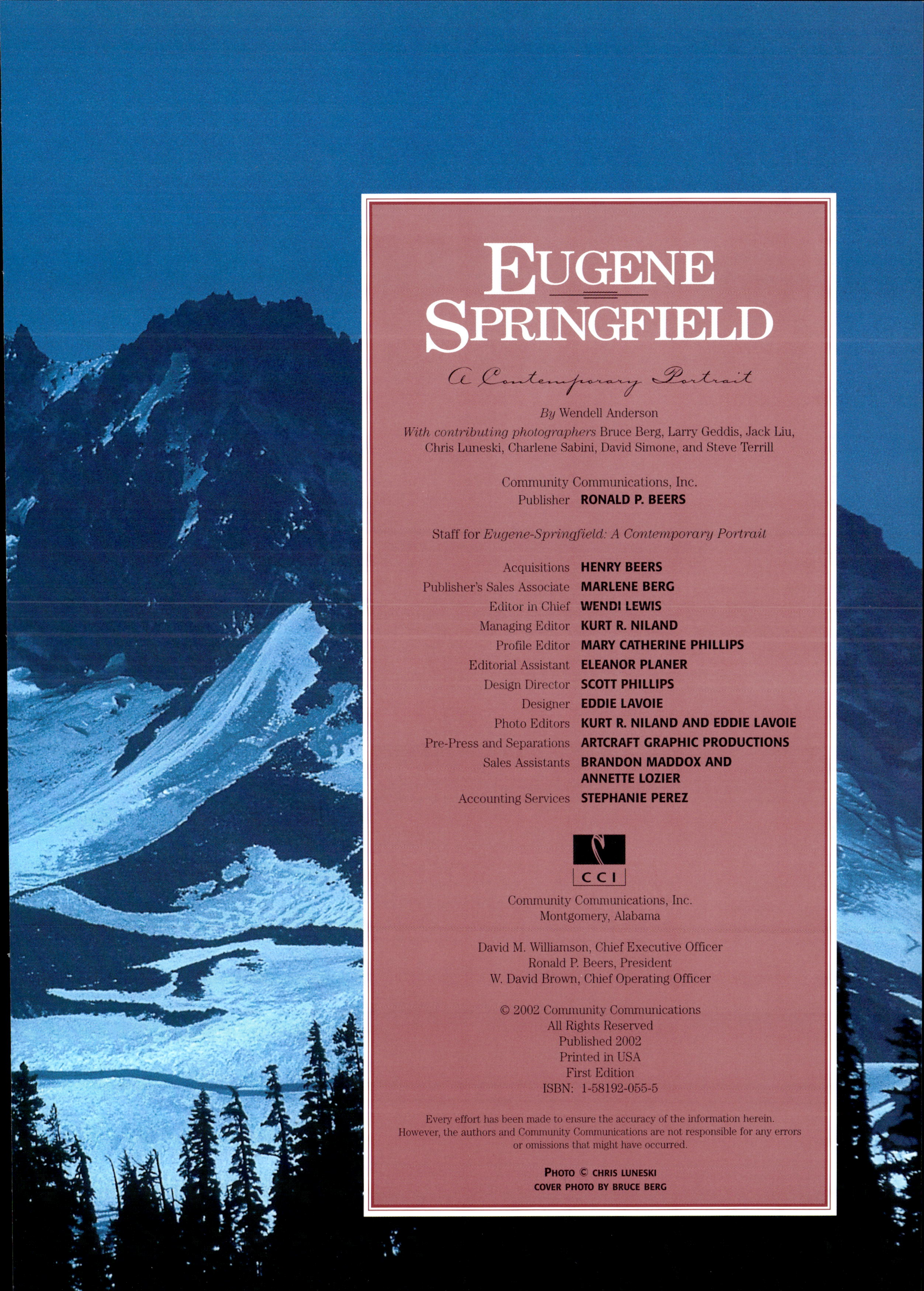

# EUGENE SPRINGFIELD

*A Contemporary Portrait*


*By* Wendell Anderson

*With contributing photographers* Bruce Berg, Larry Geddis, Jack Liu, Chris Luneski, Charlene Sabini, David Simone, and Steve Terrill



Community Communications, Inc.
Publisher **RONALD P. BEERS**

Staff for *Eugene-Springfield: A Contemporary Portrait*

Acquisitions **HENRY BEERS**
Publisher's Sales Associate **MARLENE BERG**
Editor in Chief **WENDI LEWIS**
Managing Editor **KURT R. NILAND**
Profile Editor **MARY CATHERINE PHILLIPS**
Editorial Assistant **ELEANOR PLANER**
Design Director **SCOTT PHILLIPS**
Designer **EDDIE LAVOIE**
Photo Editors **KURT R. NILAND AND EDDIE LAVOIE**
Pre-Press and Separations **ARTCRAFT GRAPHIC PRODUCTIONS**
Sales Assistants **BRANDON MADDOX AND ANNETTE LOZIER**
Accounting Services **STEPHANIE PEREZ**

CCI

Community Communications, Inc.
Montgomery, Alabama

David M. Williamson, Chief Executive Officer
Ronald P. Beers, President
W. David Brown, Chief Operating Officer





Published 2002
Printed in USA
First Edition
ISBN: 1-58192-055-5




**PHOTO © CHRIS LUNESKI**
**COVER PHOTO BY BRUCE BERG**

# Table of Contents

# FOREWORD

A quality, culturally diverse family environment; a winning spirit; an educational powerhouse; and an ideal home for business. That's the Eugene/Springfield area.

On behalf of the Eugene Area Chamber of Commerce and its local businesses, we present this book to the Eugene and Springfield communities.

Within these beautiful pages, it is our sincere hope that you will experience the quality, texture, and healthy pulse of these dynamic cities. We are rich in wonderful people, progressive partnerships, and exciting opportunities. As you enjoy this book, you will come to understand why our future is so bright.

With the dawning of a new century and new millennium, it's an exciting time in Eugene and Springfield. Those of us who live here know and appreciate the warmth and friendliness of our people, respect our traditions and heritage, take pride in sheer natural beauty of our surroundings, and look forward to many opportunities for a prosperous future.

We are proud to share with you a glimpse into the heart and soul of Eugene and Springfield, cities poised for remarkable successes in the new millennium and, more simply, great places to live, work, and do business. Most of all, however, Eugene/Springfield area is a place simply to enjoy.

***—The Eugene Area Chamber of Commerce***

**THE UPPER PROXY FALLS, LOCATED IN THE THREE SISTERS WILDERNESS AREA NEAR McKENZIE PASS, STANDS APPROXIMATELY 200 FEET HIGH. TOURISTS AND NATIVES ALIKE SHOULD NOT MISS THE SHORT AND EASY HIKE TO VISIT THE INSPIRING BEAUTY OF THE WATERFALL.**
**PHOTO BY LARRY GEDDIS**

# Chapter One

# 1

## *The Eclectic Flavor of Life in Eugene and Springfield*

Sitting comfortably in the Willamette Valley between the Coast Range and the Cascade Mountains, Eugene is home to the Willamette and McKenzie rivers, several parks and recreation areas, the University of Oregon, a mosaic of picturesque neighborhoods, and a thriving business community.
Photo by Bruce Berg

**ART ALLEY IN THE DOWNTOWN DEPOT DISTRICT IS SPRINGFIELD'S CELEBRATED OUTDOOR ART GALLERY. MURALS PAINTED BY LOCAL ARTISTS, SUCH AS THIS JESSIE BOSTELLE MEMORIAL MURAL, DECORATE THE WALLS OF MANY OF THE BUILDINGS IN THE AREA, WITH SUBJECTS THAT RANGE FROM PURE WHIMSY TO HERITAGE PRIDE. PHOTO BY DAVID SIMONE**

It's not true that it rains all the time in Eugene and Springfield, Oregon. The rainy season lasts only from January 1 to December 31.

That's one of the many jokes about the weather that the citizens of the "Emerald Empire" accept with good humor. In fact, most relish a good rain joke. "Oregonians don't tan; they rust," people say. They also say, "You can't let a little rain stop you."

Rain is a fact of life throughout the Pacific Northwest. The Eugene-Springfield area averages about 46 inches a year. December is the wettest month, July the driest.

Eugene and Springfield lay in the Willamette Valley between the Coast Range and the Cascade Mountains. Weather patterns influenced by the Pacific Ocean create a temperate climate. The average high temperature in January in Eugene and Springfield is 46 degrees, in August, 81 degrees. Some winter snows may fall on the valley floor, and some summer temperatures may reach 100 degrees. But, overall, the climate is mild with few extremes.

The moderate conditions are ideal for growing such agriculture commodities as grass seed, mint, and filberts (known elsewhere as hazelnuts). Wild blackberries and domestic strawberries, raspberries, blueberries, and marionberries, a local variety of blackberry, abound. Local backyard gardeners—and there are many—cultivate everything from azaleas to zinnias, apricots to zucchini.

The agreeable climate is just one of the many appeals of this lush and lovely corner of western Oregon.

The first visitors to the Willamette Valley were Kalapuya Indians, who settled-in some 10,000 years ago. The Kalapuya were mostly a peaceful tribe of semi-nomadic hunters and gatherers. The first Europeans to visit the valley were trappers from John Jacob Astor's Pacific Fur Company in 1812.

Eugene Skinner, originally from New York, was among the first party of eastern pioneers to settle the area. He built his cabin near a river at the foot of a low hill called *Ya-po-ah* by the Indians. That river is now called the Willamette. That hill is now known as Skinner's Butte and is part of one of the 50 or so city parks of Eugene.

Unlike most of his neighbors who caught "Oregon Fever" in the 1840s and moved west for the free farmland, Skinner intended to lay out a new town and parcel off his 320-acre claim. His plan succeeded. A town called Skinner's Landing—and sometimes Skinner's Mud Hole—grew up along the Willamette River. The city was incorporated and renamed Eugene City in 1862. Two years later, a city charter renamed it again, City of Eugene.

Three miles down river from Skinner's cabin, near the confluence of the Willamette and McKenzie Rivers, Elias and Mary Briggs of Virginia built their home in 1849 and called it Springfield after a bubbling spring on their claim. The city was platted in 1856 and incorporated in 1885.

Together, the cities of Eugene (population about 145,500) and Springfield (population about 54,000) cover some 53 square miles and comprise the commercial and cultural center of Lane County. Taking into account a dozen or so neighboring towns, the entire greater metropolitan area has a population of about 285,000, the largest metropolitan area between Portland and Sacramento. The region is large enough to be diverse and exciting, yet small enough to be friendly and relaxed.

Recent residential, commercial, and industrial development have attracted new residents and businesses and infused a new energy. Two major regional shopping centers—Valley River Center in Eugene and Gateway Mall in Springfield—plus a mixture of specialty malls and unique stores attract shoppers from all over western Oregon. The Eugene Airport is a major regional hub. Three daily Amtrak trains stop at the Eugene Depot. Interstate 5, a direct north-south commercial artery, brings commerce and visitors to the area.

Visitors can see traces of Eugene and Springfield's past in some of the cities' unique neighborhoods. Near the site of Eugene Skinner's first cabin sits The East Skinner Butte Historic District, a charming old neighborhood that includes some two-dozen buildings dating from the 1850s to the 1920s. One of the most magnificent is the aristocratic Shelton-McMurphey-Johnson house built in 1888. Known as "the castle on the hill" in its early days, the house is the epitome of Victorian architecture. It is open for tours and hosts a variety of events, from storytelling sessions to quilting demonstrations.

THE EUGENE-SPRINGFIELD AREA IS HOME TO VARIOUS CULTURAL EVENTS IN OUR LOCAL PARKS. PHOTO BY STEVE TERRILL

THE McKENZIE PASS DURING SPRINGTIME IS A WONDERFUL PLACE TO TAKE WALKS OR PICNICS AMONG THE MANY WILDFLOWERS THAT GROW IN THIS WILDERNESS AREA.
PHOTO BY BRUCE BERG

Also in Eugene is the pleasant residential neighborhood of College Hill. First plotted in the 1890s, the area was advertised as "the Nob Hill of Eugene." Developed between 1900 and 1925, the neighborhood still contains many fine examples of homes built in the Bungalow and Revival styles of that era. Most of the homes in the neighborhood stand on their original 60x150-foot lots. With its historic and newer family homes, well-kept gardens and lawns, playgrounds and pocket parks, College Hill remains one of Eugene's most desirable neighborhoods.

There's a bit of everything in downtown Eugene. Municipal, county, and federal government offices are all within the downtown core. The Hilton Eugene and Conference Center hosts visitors and meetings from around the world. While several regional financial institutions are headquartered downtown, small service firms are the mainstays of the district. A new library and new urban townhouses help to vitalize the neighborhood. The Hult Center for the Performing Arts features local and international performers. Community theaters, art galleries, jazz clubs, coffee houses, brewpubs, and specialty shops of all kinds attract visitors and locals, alike. And there are restaurants. From supper club extravagance to sidewalk cafe casual, from teashops to hot dog carts, there is something for every taste.

The Washburne Historic District, listed on the National Register of Historic Places, is a well-preserved model of an early working-class neighborhood. Recalling Springfield's glory days as a thriving mill town, the thirty-three city blocks of the district contain some 130 homes built between 1890 and 1940. Included are superb examples of the Craftsman, Mill Cottage, Traditional Box, and Homestead styles of family homes.

The Springfield Depot District is a classic American downtown. Along its main street—actually named Main Street—are antique and speciality shops, old-fashioned diners and modern restaurants, museums and art galleries, and the city's famous wall murals. The district also contains historic sites, including a short railroad siding and the restored 1891 Southern Pacific Railroad Depot, home to the Springfield Area Chamber of Commerce.

Modern commercial and industrial Springfield is concentrated in the bustling Gateway District, north of downtown. The area is home to high-tech and manufacturing firms. A dozen hotels, the largest concentration of lodging between Seattle and San Francisco, have sprung up in recent years. Visitors and residents alike enjoy shopping, entertainment at several movie complexes, and dining at dozens of restaurants.

The Eugene-Springfield area is dynamic and growing, yet it somehow manages to avoid many of the usual big city woes. The pace of life is easy. Crime rates are low. And gridlock is unheard of. A ten-minute delay is considered a traffic jam.

But it's the people, not the infrastructure, that define a place. Neither Eugene nor Springfield has ethnic neighborhoods as such. Most neighborhoods are a mixture of races and ages. The majority of people trace their roots to Europe, but growing and active Hispanic and Asian communities are adding to the ethnic mix.

The people of Eugene and Springfield are vocal, active, independent, and serious about important issues. At the same time, they are free-spirited and playful.

Both Eugene and Springfield's city governments operate under a charter that can be changed only by the voters. Both governments are directed by an elected mayor and council that appoint a city manager who is in charge of city departments and staffs. The citizens set most policies.

Whether the situation is political, environmental, or cultural, people are ready and willing to discuss the issues at public meetings, through volunteer committees, and in the mainstream and alternative media. The debate can get spirited at times, yet a strong sense of community endures.

And a strong sense of fun. Eugene and Springfield both have their eccentric sides. What city elects a Slug Queen at its annual civic celebration? Eugene. What city erects a Nutty Kingdom during its annual civic celebration? Springfield.

Whatever the political belief, there is one "neighborhood" where everyone hangs out: the great outdoors. Eugene and Springfield are ideally located in the middle of a large natural recreation area. An hour's drive to the west is the playground of the Pacific Coast where one can watch whales frolic, fish for salmon and crab, and explore

VISITORS AND RESIDENTS OF THE EUGENE-SPRINGFIELD AREA WHO ARE LOOKING FOR SOME REST AND RELAXATION CAN ENJOY THE LAKES AND STREAMS OF THE CASCADE MOUNTAINS. PHOTO © CHRIS LUNESKI

AUTUMN BEAUTY ABOUNDS IN EUGENE'S MANY PARKS. PHOTO BY LARRY GEDDIS

vast sand dunes on foot or horseback. An hour's drive to the east stand the grand Cascade Mountains, where fun lovers can ski, hike alpine trails, and raft some of the wildest rivers in the West.

The cities of Eugene and Springfield maintain public boat landings; more than 300 miles of walking, running, and bike paths; and specialty parks.

No matter where you travel in Eugene or Springfield, you'll be awed by the natural and man-made beauty. You'll encounter people with a deep respect for nature, quietly pursuing the good life in their own way. And sometimes you'll run into rain. But don't think of it as rain; think of it as liquid sunshine. □

(RIGHT) LANE COUNTY AND THE SURROUNDING AREA ARE FULL OF MOUNTAINOUS WILDERNESS; MT. BACHELOR IN NEARBY DESCHUTES COUNTY IS A POPULAR AND EASILY ACCESSIBLE SKIING AREA FOR EUGENEANS. PHOTO BY BRUCE BERG

(BELOW) THE ICY, CRYSTAL WATERS OF THE McKENZIE RIVER RUSH OUT OF THE HIGH CASCADES. PHOTO © CHRIS LUNESKI

Photo © Chris Luneski

Along the west slopes of central Oregon's Cascade Mountain Range, the wild and scenic McKenzie River rushes through the Willamette National Forest and Lane County. Photo by Larry Geddis

A KALEIDOSCOPE OF MOUNTAINS, VALLEYS, FARMS, AND RIVERS FORM THE PASTORAL LANDSCAPES SURROUNDING EUGENE. SUCH PROFOUND NATURAL VISTAS IMPART A "DOWN TO EARTH" PERSONALITY ON THE CITY AND ITS PEOPLE. PHOTOS BY BRUCE BERG

In the past Eugene was known as "Skinner's Landing," "Skinner's Mud Hole," "Eugene City," and "City of Eugene." Recently it's been called "Oz on Earth," the "Emerald City," "Tree Town U.S.A.," and "Track Town U.S.A." Whatever it's called, Eugene remains a distinctive, sometimes quirky, yet highly livable place blessed with a mild climate and matchless natural beauty. Photo by Charlene Sabini

EUGENEANS TAKE PRIDE IN THEIR HOME, AND THIS CAN BE SEEN AND FELT IN THE MANICURED LAWNS AND WELCOMING ATMOSPHERE OF EUGENE'S NEIGHBORHOODS. PHOTO BY STEVE TERRILL

The Eugene-Springfield area is proud of its Native American heritage and holds a two-day extravaganza, celebrating traditions every September by honoring past and present Native American cultures. Photos by Bruce Berg

(Opposite) Springtime brings blooming trees and the opportunity to take a walk in the sunshine. Photo © Chris Luneski

# Chapter Two

2

*Body, Mind & Spirit*

Well-rounded communities create well-rounded individuals. Eugene's educational community, its network of healthcare services and hospitals, and its religions and spiritual dimension nurture the whole individual by providing one of the nation's most admired quality of life standards. Photo © Chris Luneski

The good life for people in the Eugene-Springfield area embodies more than abundance and recreation. The good life is also expressed through the peace of mind that comes from individual health and spiritual growth, community tolerance and caring, and knowledge and education.

Peace of mind begins with health. The Oregon Legislature, along with private health-care providers and insurance carriers, has enacted a series of laws and recommendations known collectively as the Oregon Health Plan. While still a work in progress, the Oregon Health Plan's goal is to provide universal health care for all Oregonians.

The Eugene-Springfield area benefits from some of the finest health-care facilities in the country, including two hospitals.

McKenzie-Willamette Hospital, near downtown Springfield, is a locally owned, locally run, non-for-profit 114-bed facility. Modern and dynamic, McKenzie-Willamette offers a contemporary soothing decor. The hospital provides emergency services, occupational health services, a birth center, community health library and home health and hospice services.

PeaceHealth, a regional healthcare organization founded by the Sisters of St. Joseph of Peace, operates Sacred Heart Medical Center. The 432-bed, non-for-profit hospital provides a full range of healthcare services, including emergency services, open-heart surgery, neonatal intensive care and pediatric units, inpatient rehabilitation, and home health and hospice.

A number of specialized clinics and health-care facilities also help promote health and wellness. For example, Whitebird Clinic in Eugene is a full-service clinic offering low-cost health care to the entire community. The Eugene Hearing and Speech Center is the region's top facility for children and adults with hearing problems. Serenity Lane, founded and headquartered in Eugene, is a private, not-for-profit treatment center for alcoholism and drug abuse. Its program is considered one of the most effective and progressive in the country. There are also clinics that specialize in family planning, allergies and asthma, women's health, and health care for veterans.

Additionally, some 800 physicians, dentists, and mental-health specialists in private practice provide the full range of health care from traditional to alternative.

Alternative medicine, in fact, is widely practiced and accepted in Eugene and Springfield. Massage therapists, acupuncturists, herbalists, and naturopaths enjoy successful practices in the area. Once a year they and other practitioners from throughout North America come together in Eugene for the annual Health & Well-being Celebration. Past notables at the convention have included Jean Houston and Deepak Chopra.

For many people in western Oregon, fitness is the path to health. Easy access to the region's natural wonders provides ample opportunity to pursue the active outdoor life.

Closer to home, bicycling and running—two hugely popular pastimes—help many people keep fit. Eugene, with its miles of bike paths and designated bike routes along city streets, is a bicycle-friendly city. *Bicycling* magazine, in fact, rates Eugene as one of the top 10 cycling communities in the country. Eugene is also known as "Track Town U.S.A." The city and surrounding area contain numerous well-groomed running paths and trails through a variety of urban and rural landscapes. Also, each year there are plenty of fun runs and serious meets to fulfill the casual jogger and competitive athlete alike.

In addition, a number of family gyms, health clubs, martial arts schools, dance schools, and city-sponsored recreational facilities cater to fitness enthusiasts.

The spiritual life in Eugene and Springfield is evident in many and diverse forms. Perhaps the awe-inspiring natural beauty of the region evokes spiritual feelings. Certainly, local people's celebrated tolerance allows everyone to worship in church, mosque, temple, home, or grove as they choose.

The local church directory lists houses for Catholics, Eastern Orthodox, and most

PEACEHEALTH NURSES ARE ALWAYS READY WITH A WARM SMILE AND GENTLE HUG. PHOTO COURTESY OF PEACEHEALTH

THE EUGENE-SPRINGFIELD AREA HOSTS SEVERAL BICYCLE RACES AND EVENTS THROUGHOUT THE YEAR.
PHOTO © CHRIS LUNESKI

Protestant denominations. There are also a number of nondenominational and interdenominational Christian churches. Communities of Mormons, Mennonites, and Friends live and worship in the area. Sizable and active Jewish, Buddhist, and Sikh communities practice their beliefs. And followers of astrology, Wicca, Religious Science, and other alternative and New Age religions and philosophies add to the spiritual mix.

The spiritual nature of people in Eugene and Springfield is further reflected through a tradition of activism and community service. Local residents donate a lot of time and money to help each other, the country, and the planet. TheLane, a Web site database, provides information on more than 960 programs offering services to the local community and the greater world. The diversity and generosity of the community is expressed through such programs as:

- United Way
- Food for Lane County
- Friends of Public Broadcasting
- H.I.V. Alliance
- Lane County Audubon Society
- Neighborhood Economic Development Corporation
- Religious Response Network
- Northwest Coalition for Alternatives to Pesticides
- Success by 6

The spirit of tolerance, caring, and activism, strong in the Eugene-Springfield area, helps to assure that everyone participates in the good life.

The good life in Eugene and Springfield also involves exercise for the mind. In Eugene, some 35 percent of the population has completed four or more years of college. Higher education is among the top three employers in Lane County.

Strolling across the University of Oregon campus in Eugene, you notice first the trees. Towering trees, flowering trees, cowering trees. Trees with jagged or smooth leaves, white or red bark, beefy or delicate trunks. Planted to beautify the 280-acre campus, the trees, along with the open quads, give the campus the air of a refined old city park.

Besides softening the cityscape and providing a living laboratory for students in biology, botany, urban planning, and landscape architecture, the trees deposit oxygen into the air, which contributes to the health

**PHOTO BY BRUCE BERG**

of the planet. The campus trees are only one of the many contributions the university has made, and continues to make, to the Eugene-Springfield community and the world beyond.

The University of Oregon was created by an act of the Oregon Legislature in 1872. Classes began in 1876 when Deady Hall, the school's first building, was erected. A second building, Villard Hall, was completed in 1886. Both buildings, still functioning, are on the National Register of Historic Places.

From the outset, the university presented learning, culture, and diversion to the community. A baseball team, organized in 1877, and, shortly thereafter, a glee club and debating society entertained and educated townsfolk.

The first three-man faculty was led by president John M. Johnson.

Current president Dave Frohnmayer, known and respected for his many public and private contributions, took office in 1994. Before that, he served as dean of the University of Oregon Law School, and before that, he served 11 years as Oregon's attorney general.

One of only 61 universities and colleges in the United States chosen for membership in the prestigious Association of American Universities, the University of Oregon is recognized for its contributions to knowledge, community service, and athletics. Some 17,000 students from all over the world matriculate in more than 110 programs within the college of arts and sciences and six professional schools: architecture, business, journalism, education, law, and music. The university also supports 15 research institutes and centers.

Research and training are the foundations of the university. Among many outstanding programs, several stand out for their service to the community or for their contributions to the world's store of knowledge:

- The Institute of Molecular Biology is respected worldwide for its groundbreaking research and education in contemporary molecular biology.
- The James H. Warsaw Sports Marketing Center focuses on the business aspect of sports, training students in the growing field of sports marketing.
- The Institute for a Sustainable Environment investigates the ways that human forces are transforming the biophysical world.
- The Institute for Community Arts Studies, through research and education, bolsters community arts programs throughout the world.
- The Community Outreach Partnership Center helps to forge partnerships between residents of low-income housing communities and local agencies and assistance organizations.
- The Lundquist Center for Entrepreneurship develops the next generation of business leaders through education and a highly regarded internship program that supplies interns to Oregon businesses.

A number of the university's 157,000 graduates have left their individual marks in various fields. Some examples are:

- In the sciences: Orin Stafford, a chemist, developed the charcoal briquette. Two graduates have been awarded Nobel Prizes: Walter Brattain, in 1956 for his work on semiconductors and the transistor effect, and William Parry Murphy, in 1934 for his work on the treatment of anemia.

- In arts and entertainment: Thomas Hardy created the artwork for the Presidential Seal. Gladys Stone Wright was the first woman inducted into the National Band Association Hall of Fame. Actors Lindsay Wagner, Howard Hessman, and Edgar Buchanan, and movie director James Ivory are all UO alumni.
- In business: Bill Bowerman developed the waffled-soled sports shoe and, along with fellow grad Phillip Knight, founded Nike, Inc.
- In public service: Wayne Morse served 24 years in the United States Senate. Neil Goldschmidt served as governor of Oregon and secretary of transportation under President Jimmy Carter.

The university's contributions don't end with its research, training, and notable alumni. Through its extensive library system —the largest in the state—the university

(RIGHT) **ON THE FOURTH OF JULY, THOUSANDS COME TO CELEBRATE THE INDEPENDENCE OF THE UNITED STATES AT SPRINGFIELD'S ANNUAL PARADE. PHOTO BY BRUCE BERG**

(BELOW) **EXCELLENT MEDICAL FACILITIES, A GENTLE CLIMATE, SAFE STREETS, AND FRIENDLY, CARING PEOPLE MAKE THE EUGENE-SPRINGFIELD AREA WELL-SUITED FOR RETIREMENT LIVING—WITH AN EMPHASIS ON *LIVING*. PHOTO BY STEVE TERRILL**

furnishes vast and varied resources to students and investigators around the world.

Among the library's special collections, some are very special indeed.

- The Oregon Collection contains books and other materials about Oregon and by Oregon authors, including the papers of writers Ken Kesey and Ursula LeGuinn.
- The Burgess Manuscript Collection comprises 34 western European manuscripts and 25 near-Eastern manuscripts, 29 of which date from the Middle Ages or Renaissance.
- The Jane Grant Collection contains the papers of the women's rights leader and co-founder of *The New Yorker* magazine.
- The Cole Collection includes books, pamphlets, and artifacts relating to lighter-than-air craft.
- The Haycox Collection contains the former personal library of Western writer Ernest Haycox.
- The Doris Ulmann Collection includes much of the best work done by the famous photographer.
- And there are collections of materials printed in the artificial language Esperanto, books less than 5 inches high, and pulp magazines from the 1930s through 1960s.

Most of the library system's 2.5 million books; 270,000 maps; 2,700 atlases; 500,000 aerial photographs; 125,000 photographs; 6,000 videotapes and videodiscs; 100 Oregon, 35 domestic, and 55 international newspapers; 16,000 current magazines and journals; and other materials are available to the public through special viewing rooms and online catalogs.

That includes some 30,000 music scores and parts from the University of Oregon

(BELOW) **WITH WALKING, RUNNING, SKATING, AND BICYCLING PATHS IN ALMOST EVERY PARK IN THE EUGENE-SPRINGFIELD AREA, THERE'S AN OUTDOOR ACTIVITY FOR EVERYONE TO ENJOY. PHOTO BY CHARLENE SABINI**

Water sports are a favorite of Eugeneans, and there are many lakes and rivers only a short drive from the city. Photo by Steve Terrill

Photo © Chris Luneski

School of Music library. The School of Music—a true local treasure—is one of the largest and best-equipped music institutions in the western United States. More than 20 instrumental and vocal ensembles—everything from a Baroque string quarter to a modern jazz choir—give public performances throughout the year. The School of Music offers some 200 musical events annually, including performances by faculty artists, faculty ensembles, and numerous guest artists.

The famed Oregon Bach Festival, one of the premier summer music festivals in the world, and the Eugene Symphony, a professional orchestra, trace their origins to the University of Oregon School of Music.

A major contributor to the richness of the Eugene-Springfield arts scene is the University of Oregon Museum of Art. The museum was erected in 1932 to house the Murray Warner Collection of Asian Art, more than 3,000 works given to the state of Oregon by Gertrude Bass Warner. Over the years the museum's Asian and other collections have expanded to more than 12,500 objects and include Russian icons, photography, and works by contemporary Northwest artists.

The museum building, designed by former dean of architecture Ellis Lawrence, stands alone as a work of art. Its design incorporates Persian-influenced mosaic brickwork into its windowless exterior; decorative moldings, iron grillwork, and artificial skylights in its interior spaces; and a serene courtyard complete with fishpond. The museum, listed on the National Register for Historic Places, is one of the most distinctive buildings in Oregon.

The university theater also contributes to local cultural enrichment. Performances by student actors at the Robinson Theatre include everything from Restoration comedies to one-act dramas by modern playwrights.

University of Oregon sports teams, nicknamed the Ducks, provide more than mere entertainment to the fans of the "Emerald Empire." Sports at the UO evoke pride and passion in Oregonians from Ashland to Astoria. The athletes become local celebrities and cherished heroes, even after they've

**Eugene's spiritual dimension has many faces, from the fellowship of a communal church service to a quiet day fly fishing one of the local rivers.**
**(Top) photo by Bruce Berg**
**(Left) photo © Chris Luneski**

left the Eugene campus. Revenue brought in by visiting teams and fans and the merchandising of Duck souvenirs invigorate the local economy. And the selling of TV and radio rights to games helps fund university programs.

In the autumn, Pacific-10 Conference football reigns supreme. The Ducks have been a college football powerhouse in recent years, and every home game sells out. The Ducks' biggest rival is the Beavers of Oregon State University, just 40 miles north on Highway 99. Their big game every year is dubbed "The Civil War."

In winter, basketball is king—or queen. Women's basketball, in particular, is a hugely popular draw, thanks in large part to superb athletes and a winning program.

In spring, a young man's and young woman's fancy turns to track. The University of Oregon is one the top track schools in the country and continually turns out world-class athletes. Steve Prefontaine, the legendary runner of the 1970s, is perhaps the track program's best-known star.

Other stars who have distinguished themselves on UO fields and courts include Bev Smith, Hall of Fame basketball player; professional football players Dan Fouts, Chris Miller, Norm Van Brocklin, and Ahmad Rashad, now a sportscaster for NBC; Peter Jacobson, professional golfer; Alberto Salazar and Kelly Blair, track stars; and Terrell Brandon, NBA all-star.

One UO team holds a special place in college sports history. The 1939 basketball team won the first ever NCAA basketball championship. Members of that team were nicknamed the "Tall Firs." In a community that loves its trees, such a nickname confers the highest homage.

But Eugeneans can devour knowledge through means other than education. Entrance to the world's store of knowledge is available through several fine libraries. The extensive University of Oregon library system, the largest in the state, is open to the community, and the city of Springfield Public Library includes among its services weekly story hours for children, computer workstations, and public Internet access.

But the crown jewel of local libraries is the new downtown Eugene Public Library, built with public and private funds. No dusty, musty quiet mausoleum, the Eugene Public Library is a bustling place, a crossroads, and one of the anchors in downtown Eugene's recent redevelopment. More than 12,000 patrons visit the library every week. Some 80 percent of Eugene households hold active library cards. Eugeneans check out about 11.2 items per person per year, about twice the national average.

Other storehouses of knowledge in the Eugene-Springfield area include an assortment of specialty museums. The Springfield Museum exhibits pictures and artifacts of life in early Oregon. The Lane County

**Springfield City Hall. Photo by Charlene Sabini**

PHOTO BY BRUCE BERG

Historical Museum in Eugene holds a vast collection of materials depicting Lane County's history from the early 1800s to the present. The University of Oregon Museum of Natural History includes mounted displays and programs on the natural sciences and native cultures. The Oregon Air & Space Museum, near the Eugene Airport, contains a squadron of aircraft, everything from a World War I triplane to supersonic fighters; historic aviation artifacts, including uniforms and flight suits; an extensive scale model collection; and more. The Willamette Science and Technology Center explores and explains the sciences, from math to engineering, through its rotating displays. The Lane Education Service District Planetarium offers laser shows and a variety of special shows all relating to astronomical events.

An active media keep local residents abreast of international, national, and local events. The two chief newspapers are *The Register-Guard*, Eugene's award-winning daily newspaper, and *Springfield News*, a semiweekly journal. Other local print media includes *Eugene Weekly*, the area's alternative newspaper and *Comic News*, a compendium of political cartoons and social satire.

Radio is a popular medium in Eugene and Springfield for information and entertainment. Some 30 stations—a large number for a market the size of Lane County—fill the airwaves with talk shows, public affairs programming, and music of all kinds. Listeners support four public radio stations, including KWAX, one of the few stations in the country with an all-classical music format. □

THE FIRE DEPARTMENTS OF BOTH EUGENE AND SPRINGFIELD WORK AROUND THE CLOCK TO KEEP THE COMMUNITIES AS SAFE AS POSSIBLE. PHOTO BY BRUCE BERG

THE NEW EUGENE PUBLIC LIBRARY WILL OPEN EARLY 2003. IT PLAYS A ROLE IN EUGENE'S DOWNTOWN AS A FORCE FOR DOWNTOWN REVITALIZATION, A COMMUNITY GATHERING PLACE, AND A PUBLIC FORUM. PHOTO BY CHARLENE SABINI

CREATED BY AN ACT OF THE OREGON LEGISLATURE IN 1872, THE UNIVERSITY OF OREGON HAS BEEN THE CORNERSTONE OF THE COMMUNITY SINCE THE FIRST CLASSES WERE OFFERED IN 1876. PHOTO BY JACK LIU

SOME 17,000 STUDENTS FROM ALL OVER THE WORLD MATRICULATE IN MORE THAN 110 PROGRAMS WITHIN THE COLLEGE OF ARTS AND SCIENCES AND SIX PROFESSIONAL SCHOOLS: ARCHITECTURE, BUSINESS, JOURNALISM, EDUCATION, LAW, AND MUSIC. PHOTO BY JACK LIU

*"Eugene's community proudly boasts its reputation of placing a high value on education, providing an unparalled variety of the arts and being 'the home of the Ducks.' But in the final analysis, it is the warm people of Eugene, who will welcome you and entice you to make it your home."*

**GEORGE MCCULLY, DMD**
*Managing Partner*
*Spencer View Dental Park*

STROLLING ACROSS THE UNIVERSITY OF OREGON CAMPUS IN EUGENE, YOU NOTICE FIRST THE TREES. PLANTED TO BEAUTIFY THE 280-ACRE CAMPUS. THE TREES, ALONG WITH THE OPEN QUADS, GIVE THE CAMPUS THE AIR OF A REFINED OLD CITY PARK. PHOTO BY JACK LIU

RESEARCH AND TRAINING ARE THE FOUNDATIONS OF THE UNIVERSITY, WHICH EVERY YEAR GRADUATES GROUND-BREAKING LEADERS IN THE SCIENCES, ART, AND BUSINESS. PHOTO BY JACK LIU

(LEFT) WHILE STEEPED IN HISTORY, THE UNIVERSITY OF OREGON IS TODAY A PIONEER OF THE FUTURE WITH ITS CUTTING-EDGE RESEARCH IN BIOTECHNOLOGY, MOLECULAR BIOLOGY, BIOPHYSICS, AND OTHER SCIENCES OF DISCOVERY. PHOTO BY JACK LIU

(BELOW) UNIVERSITY OF OREGON SPORTS TEAMS, NICKNAMED THE DUCKS, PROVIDE MORE THAN MERE ENTERTAINMENT TO THE FANS OF THE "EMERALD EMPIRE." SPORTS AT THE UO EVOKE PRIDE AND PASSION IN OREGONIANS FROM ASHLAND TO ASTORIA. PHOTO BY JACK LIU

One of only 61 universities and colleges in the United States chosen for membership in the prestigious Association of American Universities, the University of Oregon is recognized for its contributions to knowledge, community service, and athletics. Photos by Jack Liu

# Chapter Three

# 3

## A Growing Economy

While it used to be in reign of a steady logging industry, Eugene experienced the usual pains that come with economic diversification. Now, with an edge on high-technology, Eugene's economy hasn't merely kept pace with the demands of today, it has grown to fulfill the visions of tomorrow. Photo by Bruce Berg

AGRICULTURE, ONE OF THE THREE PRINCIPAL INDUSTRIES IN LANE COUNTY, BRINGS IN REVENUES OF CLOSE TO $90,000,000. PHOTOS BY STEVE TERRILL

In August, an intense herbal aroma surges from fields north of Eugene and Springfield. The fumes can be quite heady and even make the eyes water at times. But the odor is always fresh, brisk, and pleasantly earthy.

Farmers are harvesting their mint crop and distilling it to make oil to flavor candy, toothpaste, medicines, and other minty concoctions. Mint is one of the important products of one of Lane County's important industries: agriculture.

Since the early days of Eugene and Springfield in the 1840s, agriculture has been a major economic force. It was, after all, the free fertile land that first attracted pioneer farmers to the Willamette Valley. They discovered that the soil and climate were ideal for growing wheat and other cereal crops.

As more farmers moved into the valley, the inventory of crops grew to include flax, hops, alfalfa, tree fruits, berries, nuts—and mint. Oliver Hovey Todd introduced mint to the area in 1908. These crops and others flourished and helped to establish agriculture as one of the engines that drives the local economy.

In 1851 a natural event occurred that fired up another economic engine and determined the future of the Eugene-Springfield area. That event was a flood. In the winter of 1851, after heavy rains, the Willamette River overflowed its banks, destroying new homes and farms. But disaster for some people was opportunity for others. Several entrepreneurs recognized, naturally enough, the power of the river and sought to exploit it. They also noticed the natural channels carved out by the floodwaters.

Near the fledgling town of Skinner's Landing (later renamed Eugene), Hilyard Shaw scooped out the natural channel further to create a millrace, a diversion in the river. Shortly after, he built a sawmill and gristmill. At about the same time at a spot several miles downstream where Springfield now stands, Elias and Isaac Briggs also turned a meandering channel into a millrace. Soon after they and their partners erected a sawmill and flourmill.

The economic course was set. By 1870, there were at least 18 gristmills, wool mills, and—most important—sawmills along the banks of the Willamette and McKenzie rivers. Even though agriculture remained vital to the local economy, lumber ruled for the next 125 years.

Loggers (don't call them "lumberjacks") harvested countless millions of trees from the vast, seemingly endless forests of fir, pine, and oak of the Pacific Northwest. At first, they floated logs down the rivers to

PHOTO BY BRUCE BERG

the mills in Springfield and Eugene. Then in 1871 the railroad arrived from Portland. Raw timber moved into the mill towns by rail, and processed lumber and wood products moved out.

A thriving industry flourished around lumber. Jobs were plentiful in the woods, sawmills, wood-product manufacturing plants, glue and resin factories, supply and outfitting stores, railroad yards, and trucking firms. Times were good. Everyone worked. Even the Great Depression of the 1930s couldn't slow down King Lumber. Springfield, in particular, prospered, thanks to the world's constant need for wood and wood products.

Then in the 1970s and '80s, environmental and market forces combined to alter forever the natural and economic landscape. The Endangered Species Act of 1973 forced a change in logging practices. A slowdown in construction fomented by the recession of the 1980s brought King Lumber to his knees. The decline in the forest products industry meant hard times for the people of Eugene and Springfield.

But now, thanks to economic diversification, recovery is complete. Today, Eugene and Springfield enjoy a bustling economy no longer dependent on one industry.

Four local organizations have been especially effectual in developing the new economy of Eugene and Springfield. The Eugene-Springfield Metropolitan Partnership works with recruitment and expansion businesses. The Business Development Center of Lane Community College provides business education to small businesses and encourages entrepreneurship. The Eugene Area Chamber of Commerce promotes business success through business assistance, advocacy of public policy, and community development. The Convention and Visitors Association of Lane County promotes tourism.

Tourism is now one of the three principal industries in the county, along with education and agriculture. And while agriculture

**High-tech manufacturers such as Sony Disc Manufacturing, Symantec Corporation, and PSC Scanning employ several hundred workers. Photo by Steven Duffey**

accounts for a large portion of the revenues for the area, it accounts for about only 9 percent of the total labor force.

The service sector—which includes professional, business, and health services—accounts for about 24 percent of jobs in the area. Growth of the service sector demonstrates the success of economic diversification.

While some service providers employ hundreds of workers, such as Oregon Medical Laboratories, SELCO Credit Union, and Goodwill Industries, most service businesses—as well as manufacturing and retail businesses—are small businesses. Most of the area's 10,000 or so businesses, in fact, employ fewer than 20 workers and make up the heart of the local economy.

TRANSPORTATION IS ALWAYS A BOOSTER FOR THE LOCAL ECONOMY, AIDING EACH INDUSTRY BY TRANSPORTING BOTH PEOPLE AND CARGO IN AND OUT OF THE EUGENE-SPRINGFIELD AREA DAILY, THUS ENCOURAGING GROWTH AND DIVERSIFICATION IN TOURISM, AGRICULTURE, AND PRIVATE BUSINESS. PHOTOS BY BRUCE BERG

Some 23 percent of jobs in Lane County are in wholesale and retail trade. The Eugene-Springfield metropolitan area is the primary shopping center in the southern Willamette Valley, a region with a population of more than 750,000 people. Most of the well-known national retailers have at least one outlet in Eugene or Springfield: Sears Roebuck & Company, Starbucks, Safeway, Barnes & Noble, J.C. Penney, and Wal-Mart, to name a few. A number of regional retailers also operate stores in Lane County, among them Fred Meyer stores, Bi-Mart Corporation, Les Schwab Tires, Troutman's Emporium, and Euphoria Chocolates.

In addition to two major shopping centers, Valley River Center in Eugene and Gateway Mall in Springfield, the area contains a number of smaller neighborhood shopping centers. The Market District near downtown Eugene, for example, includes the Fifth Street Public Market, Fifth-Pearl Shops, and Station Square, a collection of one-of-a-kind shops and eateries. And nearly every neighborhood has its complement of independent grocers, family restaurants, bed & breakfasts, and specialty shops, selling everything from garden art to wooden toys to Mexican pastries.

Government and education also supply many jobs. Some 17 percent of jobs in Eugene and Springfield are in the public sector. Major public employers include the University of Oregon, Lane Community

College, Eugene and Springfield School Districts, Willamalane Park & Recreation District, and the United States Government.

Some remnants of the old glory days of King Lumber remain. Manufacturing still accounts for about 14 percent of jobs in the area. While a few forest product manufacturers are still major employers and key players in the local economy—most notably Weyerhaeuser Co., Rosboro Lumber Company, and States Industries, Inc—other types of manufacturers add to the economic mix of the new glory days. There are more than 800 manufacturing companies of all sizes and types in Lane County.

High-tech manufacturers such as Sony Disc Manufacturing, Symantec Corporation, and PSC Scanning employ several hundred workers. Country Coach, Inc., Marathon Coach, and Monaco Coach Corp. have made Lane County a center for recreational vehicle manufacturing. And smaller specialty manufacturers such as Custom Craftworks, Inc., maker of massage tables, and Kingsford Manufacturing Company, maker of charcoal briquettes, contribute to the diversity.

The outlook for the local economy appears promising. Jobs are expected to grow in semiconductor manufacturing, home health services, computer sciences, social welfare counseling, and childcare—a far cry from Eugene and Springfield's rough and tumble lumber past. An energetic and generally well-educated workforce (some 35 percent of people in Eugene, for example, have a college degree) help to assure a prosperous future. Leaders in government, education, business, and the environmental movement, along with Lane County citizens, are committed to managing the inevitable growth while preserving the quality of life.

Yet for the all the swings in the economy, rise and fall of industries, and shifts in attitudes, agriculture remains at the root of the local economy. Grass seeds, tree fruits, and nuts are the top three farm products in gross sales. Total sales for all crops in Lane County annually approach $90,000,000 and truly help keep the Eugene-Springfield area "in the mint." □

LOGGERS HARVESTED MILLIONS OF TREES AND FLOATED THEM DOWN THE RIVERS TO THE MILLS IN SPRINGFIELD AND EUGENE UNTIL 1871 WHEN THE RAILROAD ARRIVED FROM PORTLAND. RAW TIMBER MOVED INTO THE MILL TOWNS BY RAIL, AND PROCESSED LUMBER AND WOOD PRODUCTS MOVED OUT. PHOTO BY BRUCE BERG

THE SERVICE SECTOR—WHICH INCLUDES PROFESSIONAL, BUSINESS, AND HEALTH SERVICES—ACCOUNTS FOR ABOUT 24 PERCENT OF JOBS IN THE AREA. PHOTO BY CHARLENE SABINI

INTERSTATE 5, A VITAL NORTH-SOUTH ARTERY IN THE STATE, RUNS THROUGH THE EUGENE AREA AND PLAYS A KEY ROLE IN THE ECONOMY OF THE AREA. PHOTO BY CHARLENE SABINI

*"Sony Disc Manufacturing was attracted to this community for a number of reasons, but mostly for the area's quality of life for our employees. We believe it's our responsibility as good corporate citizens to help maintain and improve this quality of life through our direct involvement with non-profit social services and educational programs, as well as through the Chamber of Commerce and local government officials. We contribute financially and in-kind and encourage our employees to volunteer as well. In the long run, our community involvement contributes to the success of our business."*

**THOMAS COSTABILE**
*Senior Vice President*
*Operations*
*Sony Disc Manufacturing*

A THRIVING INDUSTRY FLOURISHED AROUND LUMBER, AND JOBS WERE PLENTIFUL IN THE WOODS, SAWMILLS, WOOD-PRODUCT MANUFACTURING PLANTS, GLUE AND RESIN FACTORIES, SUPPLY AND OUTFITTING STORES, RAILROAD YARDS, AND TRUCKING FIRMS. PHOTO BY BRUCE BERG

WHILE TOURISM AND TIMBER PLAY A KEY ROLE IN THE LOCAL ECONOMY, AGRICULTURE IS STILL A MAJOR SOURCE OF REVENUE FOR EUGENE. THE AREA'S TEMPERATE CLIMATE AND NOURISHING ENVIRONMENT SPELL SUCCESS FOR THE RANCHES AND FARMS. PHOTOS BY BRUCE BERG

In early years as today, the power of the McKenzie and Willamette rivers was harnessed as fuel for the Eugene-Springfield area. While the rivers are more recreational today, their role as providers of hydroelectric energy is still unmistakable, although supplementary to fossil fuels. Photo by Bruce Berg

Towering trees dominate the forests around the Eugene-Springfield area. Photo © Chris Luneski

Heavy industries, like this sand and gravel company, also thrive in resource-rich Lane County. Photo by Charlene Sabini

# Chapter Four

# 4

## Rivers Run Through It

The Willamette River and the McKenzie River, the two rivers that have figured so prominently in the life of Eugene, Springfield, and surrounding communities, are as different as ice and fire.
Photo by Charlene Sabini

The rivers of the western United States have played a major role in the natural and social history of the region. Oregon rivers—particularly the mighty Columbia, which meets the Pacific Ocean in northern Oregon—have defined the land, transported people to the West, and nourished communities.

Rivers are unlike other bodies of water. Rivers are individuals; each takes on a unique personality. The Willamette River and the McKenzie River, the two rivers that have figured so prominently in the life of Eugene, Springfield, and surrounding communities, are as different as ice and fire.

The Willamette River is an eccentric stream. The Willamette (pronounced wil-lam-'ut) is notable for its distinctions.

First of all, the Willamette has two headwater sources. The main branch, called the Middle Fork, spills from Lake Timpanogas at the foot of Cowhorn Mountain in the Cascades, about 70 miles southeast of Eugene and Springfield. Another branch, the Coast Fork, springs up somewhere farther north and west of Cowhorn. The two forks converge just south of Springfield at Dorris Ranch.

Another peculiarity: The Willamette, the 12th largest river in the United States in terms of water volume, is one of the few North American rivers that flows north. It journeys through Springfield, Eugene, Salem—Oregon's capital—and meets the Columbia River at Portland.

(Above) **The Willamette River is the 12th largest river in the United States and is one of the few North American rivers that flows north. Photo by Bruce Berg**

(Right) **The Willamette River valley is home to many trails and parks where residents and tourists can participate in dozens of outdoor activities from hiking and bird watching to boating and swimming. Photo by Larry Geddis**

Another distinction: At approximately 290 miles in length, the Willamette is the longest river in the United States to be contained in one state.

And the Willamette is one of only 14 American Heritage Rivers, a federal designation that recognizes the historic significance and current problems of the waterway. Unfortunately, the Willamette, like so many American rivers, has lost its pristine character because of increasing urbanization. The Willamette River Basin, covering just 12 percent of Oregon, is home to nearly 70 percent of the state's residents. From the early days of settlement, abuses and carelessness led to a decline in water quality.

The problems were recognized as far back as the 1920s, but it wasn't until the 1940s that citizen groups formed, in typical Oregon grassroots fashion, for the purpose of cleaning up this cherished resource. The rise of environmental consciousness in the 1970s and '80s led to further concerted efforts to clean up the Willamette. And those efforts have not ebbed. In 1999 Oregon implemented the Willamette Restoration Plan, a multiphase, long-term remediation program developed with federal assistance and managed by a diverse group of concerned environmentalists, scientists, and business people. Continual monitoring should ensure the health of the Willamette.

Although navigable through most of its course, the Willamette was a disappointing commercial route upstream near Eugene and Springfield. Further downstream near Portland, the river is wider and deeper and more adaptable to large-scale transportation. Early Lane County settlers launched steamboats on the river but found it too shallow. Specially designed shallow-draft boats plied a modest trade, but steamboat travel was very slow, taking as long as three days to cruise the 40 miles upstream from Corvallis to Eugene. The only time that most big boats could readily sail the river was when it flooded in spring, which it often did, and often with catastrophic results to the burgeoning populations in the fertile river basin.

In the 1940s the Army Corps of Engineers began building a chain of dams and reservoirs throughout the entire Willamette Basin. These dams and reservoirs harnessed the river and its tributaries for flood control, irrigation, and power production.

But the Willamette River is cherished and protected mostly for its matchless natural beauty and contribution to the Oregon way of life. Even with increased urbanization, the Willamette Basin is home or refuge to a large assortment of wildlife. Salmon and trout migrate from the Pacific Ocean and Columbia River to the Willamette and its tributaries to spawn. Numerous other native and introduced fish species, including bass, challenge fishermen. Black bear, Roosevelt elk, black-tailed deer, beaver, nutria, cougar, and other mammals dwell in and along the river. Wintering and migrating birds such as

THE McKENZIE RIVER WAS ONCE USED TO TRANSPORT LUMBER TO SAWMILLS SET ALONG THE RIVERSIDE. PHOTO BY LARRY GEDDIS

THESE DAYS THE RIVERS ARE USED FOR RECREATION AND ENJOYMENT; FROM RAFTING WHITE WATER RAPIDS TO WATER SKIING, THERE IS NO DOUBT THAT OREGONIANS LOVE WATER SPORTS. PHOTO BY BRUCE BERG

PHOTO BY STEVE TERRILL

Canada goose, pintail duck, and whistling swan rest and feed in the lakes, streams, and reservoirs of the basin.

As it courses through Springfield and Eugene, the Willamette River blends into the urban landscape. Though not a gentle stream at this point, the Willamette is, nevertheless, a central element of the parks system. Large and small parks, walkways and bikeways, and nature trails run along its banks. People also swim (with some risk), canoe, and boat in its waters. And the fishing is good from several pedestrian bridges that span the river. Very little industrial and commercial development has occurred along the Willamette in the metro area, leaving the river available to everyone.

The McKenzie River is a designated—and authentic—Wild and Scenic River. It has a bold, gregarious, in-your-face personality. The McKenzie is all about fun.

The icy, crystal waters of the McKenzie rush out of the high Cascades, plunge 5,000 feet to the valley floor, and run 85 miles westward through old-growth forests, agricultural land, and small communities. It snakes through north Springfield and joins the Willamette River in north Eugene.

"Up the McKenzie," as folks in Eugene and Springfield say, is one large natural playground. Near and along the river, fun seekers discover Sahalie Falls Park, Belknap Gardens and Hot Springs, Cougar Reservoir Recreation Area, Silver Creek wildlife viewing area, Ben and Kay Dorris State Park, Leaburg Lake Recreation Area, Armitage State Park, two fish hatcheries, and dozens of small resorts, wayside picnic areas, hiking trails, campgrounds, and boat ramps.

The McKenzie has been described as the classic western fishing river. Much of the river is open to angling year around, but May through October is high season. The stream's character in the lower section is mostly riffles and pocket water, perfect for fly-fishing from a drift boat. During the season the river is heavily stocked with planter trout. There are also good runs of summer steelhead and spring Chinook salmon. Fish range from 12 to 16 inches and possess plenty of spirit. Natives of the river include rainbow, cutthroat, bull, and the elusive redside trout. (For all native species, fish and game laws stipulate "catch and release.")

The McKenzie provides plenty of enjoyment for those who don't drown worms. The river is a boaters' nirvana. No matter what the craft—canoe, kayak, pontoon, drift boat, or raft—the McKenzie accommodates it and has done so since 1909

when Carey Thomson began hauling tourists in his McKenzie drift boat.

The McKenzie drift boat, or "square-ender," is a unique vessel designed in the early 20th century strictly for river travel. The standard Hindman boat, the most popular drift boat on the river today, was developed in the 1940s by Woodie Hindman. This boat, also called the "double-ender," has a pointed stern and flattened bow, which makes it highly maneuverable through currents and high waves.

The Hindman is the favorite craft of anglers and those who just like to float down river on a sunny afternoon and enjoy the passing scenery. The lower McKenzie has several long, peaceful stretches of 4 to 6 miles that pass through lush green forests of Douglas fir rife with wildlife.

For those who like more adventure on the water, the McKenzie has some of the most exciting river runs in Oregon. The upper McKenzie is narrow and fast with nearly continuous whitewater and Class 2, 3, and even some 3+ rapids. A number of fine whitewater rafting companies with experienced river guides provide unforgettable excursions at every level of rafting.

If you can't have fun on the McKenzie, you're just not trying.

Both the Willamette and McKenzie helped shape the cities of Eugene and Springfield. The two rivers were the first commercial arteries, particularly for loggers who floated logs down the rivers to the mills of Eugene and Springfield. The two rivers also furnished power to run the cities' industries. Now the Willamette and McKenzie are no longer commercial or industrial rivers, but recreational rivers that as much as ever help define the personalities of Eugene and Springfield. □

**THE WILLAMETTE MILL RACE IN SPRINGFIELD, DUG BY CITY FOUNDER ELIAS BRIGGS IN THE 1850S, STILL COURSES THROUGH THE CITY TODAY. PHOTO BY BRUCE BERG**

(RIGHT) THERE ARE MANY WALKING TRAILS THAT RUN RIGHT NEXT TO THE SCENIC RIVER THAT WINDS THROUGHOUT EUGENE, PROVIDING A RELAXING ATMOSPHERE AND AESTHETIC SURROUNDINGS FOR ITS RESIDENTS. PHOTO BY CHARLENE SABINI

THE NATIONAL SCENIC BYWAYS AND STATE PARKS THAT ARE ASSOCIATED WITH THE RIVERS ARE A HUGE TOURIST DRAW TO THE EUGENE-SPRINGFIELD AREA. PHOTO BY BRUCE BERG

*"Tourism in Eugene has flourished and kept up with the growth that the city has experienced in recent years. I think people come to Eugene to experience the natural beauty and warmth that the city and its landscape has to offer and in the process wins new fans in what the people of Eugene have known all along; that Eugene is one of the finest places in the country for people to live, prosper, and retire in."*

**Chris Otto**
*General Manager*
*Valley River Inn*

The Williamette and McKenzie rivers offer adventure for kayakers and other boaters.
Photo © Chris Luneski

(LEFT & OPPOSITE) **ALTON BAKER PARK OFFERS LOCAL RESIDENTS AND VISITORS ALIKE, A QUIET PLACE TO SPEND THE DAY. PHOTOS BY CHARLENE SABINI**

# Chapter Five

# 5

## *Let Us Entertain You*

Entertainment is not too hard to come by in the Eugene-Springfield area. Outdoor markets and a calendar full of festivals, as well as a full theater season, are just a few of the activities available to choose from. Photo © Chris Luneski

(ABOVE) **THE ITALS, AN AWARD-WINNING JAMAICAN REGGAE BAND, PERFORM TO AN ENTHUSIASTIC AUDIENCE AT SPRINGFIELD'S FILBERT FESTIVAL. PHOTO BY BRUCE BERG**

The people of Eugene have a good time throughout the year, day or night, rain or shine. So get out your calendars and get ready for a full year of fairs, festivals, and gala performances of all kinds.

The theater season is in full swing by January. Plays are being staged by several professional and community companies such as The Very Little Theatre in southeast Eugene, the oldest continuous running community theater in the United States. Downtown, Actors Cabaret presents revivals and original shows in an intimate club setting. Students from the University of Oregon and Lane Community College offer the full range of theatrical experiences throughout the school year.

A mixed bag of popular music is heard all year long at the Community Center for the Performing Arts, also known as the W.O.W. Hall. With its famous floating dance floor, this former Woodsmen of the World lodge is *the* spot for people of all ages to party down.

The McDonald Theatre in downtown Eugene is the area's newest performance venue. Once a classic American movie house, the McDonald Theatre has been renovated into a small concert hall and books local and national music acts of all kinds.

The first big festival of the year takes place in February at the Lane County Fairgrounds. The Oregon Asian Celebration is the longest running cultural fair in Oregon and one of Eugene's largest gatherings. For two days, the local Asian community expresses its diverse cultures through music, dance, foods, arts, and education.

The outdoor festival season begins in May with Fiesta Latina. For three days, Latin American culture holds sway with special activities for children, food, music, and lots and lots of dancing. Fiesta Latina started as a small Cinco de Mayo remembrance for Eugene's Mexican American community. It now celebrates the various cultures of Central America, South America, and the Caribbean and is one of Eugene's most exuberant and popular annual parties.

Also in May is the Willamette Valley Folk Festival on the University of Oregon Campus. Since 1970, the festival has brought together top performers of traditional and contemporary folk music and dance from around the world.

**EUGENE AND SPRINGFIELD ARE PROUD OF THEIR CULTURAL DIVERSITY AND CELEBRATE THESE DIFFERENCES WITH PERFORMANCES BY SCOTTISH BAGPIPE PLAYERS AT A LOCAL FESTIVAL. THERE ARE ALSO ANNUAL FESTIVALS AND EVENTS DEDICATED TO THE AREA'S LATIN AMERICAN, ASIAN, AND SCANDINAVIAN RESIDENTS. PHOTO BY BRUCE BERG**

The city of Florence, 60 miles west of Eugene on the Pacific Coast, salutes the "rhodie" each May during its Rhododendron Festival. The festive weekend includes 5K and 10K runs, an arts and crafts show, a queen's pageant and coronation, a motorcycle show, and—the highlight of the festival—a grand floral parade.

In June, the world comes to Eugene for the Oregon Bach Festival, truly one of the world's premiere summer music festivals. For two weeks, classical music lovers are treated to orchestral and choral music by Johann Sebastian Bach, as well as many other past and contemporary composers, performed by the world's foremost virtuosi. The festival also includes artists' recitals, master classes, lectures, and many free musical performances at a variety of venues around town.

The festival season picks ups steam in July, a busy month in Eugene. During the first weekend of the month, Alton Baker Park is the site for Art & the Vineyard, a multimedia arts festival and showcase for local fine artists and artisans. The culinary arts are represented in a food court where you can feast on unusual and eye-appealing delicacies. And more than 15 Oregon wineries host a wine tasting, offering the best of the vintner's art.

Also in July, Eugene's Japanese American community stages the Japanese Obon and Taiko Drum Festival, a traditional folk festival to honor the dead. Japanese folk dancers and taiko drum troupes from all over the Northwest and Japan assemble for this beautiful and unusual observance.

Later in the month near the town of Veneta, just west of Eugene, emerges a scene right out of the 1960s: the Oregon Country Fair, a true happening. Somewhat controversial in the past, the Oregon Country Fair has shifted its focus to

THE HULT CENTER FOR THE PERFORMING ARTS HOUSES EIGHT RESIDENT PERFORMING COMPANIES FROM A VARIETY OF DISCIPLINES, AS WELL AS THE JACOB GALLERY, WHICH FEATURES WORK FROM REGIONAL ARTISTS.
PHOTO BY BRUCE BERG

become three days of arts, foods, and vaudeville for the entire family. Yet the Oregon Country Fair remains anything but conventional.

In August the festival calendar really gets crowded. The small community of Junction City, just north of Eugene, turns into a Nordic village during the four-day Scandinavian Festival. Local residents of Swedish, Norwegian, Danish, and Finnish ancestry salute their heritages with foods, crafts, and entertainments. Everyone in town comes in old-world costume while performers from around North America and Scandinavia present traditional music and folk dances.

The city of Springfield, Eugene's neighbor, pays homage to the Official State Nut of Oregon, the filbert (known elsewhere as the hazelnut), with the annual Springfield Filbert Festival. The Filbert Festival features nonstop entertainment, fireworks, a 5K and 12K run, an old-fashioned ice cream social, a pancake breakfast, arts, crafts, and, of course, plenty of tasty foods.

In August the Oregon Festival of American Music takes over for two weeks of music, lectures, and classes. Local and national artists from the worlds of classical, jazz, folk, and popular music convene to focus on a different aspect of American musical tradition. The festival includes music camps for young artists and many free shows for the entire family.

A yearly highlight for nearly everyone is the Lane County Fair, held every August at the fairgrounds in Eugene. Pure Americana, the fair features farm, business, and technology exhibits; a large midway carnival; arts and crafts displays; local and national entertainers; and the best food this side of mom's kitchen. The Lane County Fair draws thousands of revelers and is one of Eugene's biggest annual events.

The end of summer doesn't signal the end of fun. In September, the drums welcome people to Celebrating Traditions, a two-day powwow honoring past and present Native American cultures. Arts, crafts, music, storytelling, and exhibition and social dancing round out the weekend.

No event is more quintessentially Eugene than the Eugene Celebration. For three days in September, all the zaniness, seriousness, and quirkiness of Eugeneans burst forth. The celebration is part jubilee, part exercise in civic pride, and part homage to individualism.

A highlight of the Eugene Celebration is the Grand Parade, a procession unlike any other. In addition to the traditional floats and high school marching bands, parade entries may include dance teams of beefy men in tutus; a giant ear reminding people to have their hearing checked; and a contingent from Eugene's American Hogwarts Wizardry School. The star of the parade is the Slug Queen. Her "sliminess" is elected anew each year by popular decree and reigns over the festivities.

Other events include a pet parade, bicycle races, an 8K run and walk, a kite festival, a photo contest, and the Mayor's

Festivals, fairs, and parades—there's something for everyone, including this contestant in a chili cook off.
Photo by Bruce Berg

Art Show. And of course there is food for every taste. Venues include KidZone, an area of interactive science and art projects for kids of all ages, and a half dozen performance stages featuring new vaudevillians, dancers, comedians, and musicians offering an eclectic array of music that must be heard to be appreciated.

September also marks the beginning of the season for the Eugene Ballet Company, Eugene Symphony, and Eugene Opera. Combined, these three professional companies provide more than a dozen full-scale productions of classical and contemporary works. Internationally known guest artists are often featured. Highlights of the season include the annual Holiday Pops concert, performances of the *Nutcracker* ballet, and the staging of a grand opera on New Year's Eve.

New Year's Eve also marks the end of the festival year with yet another unique Eugene bash. First Night Eugene is an alcohol-free party for families. The venue is the whole of downtown. Some 15 different visual and performing arts platforms and stages offer everything from belly dancing to square dancing, rap and hip-hop to swing and be-bop. A grand procession, open to all, opens the celebration; a huge fireworks display at midnight ends the festivities. First Night Eugene is one of the city's premier fun family events and has served as a model for similar events in other cities.

There is never a problem with keeping your social and fun calendar filled in Eugene. □

(Top) Eugeneans don't have to wait for a festival to have a good time. They can participate in one of their favorite hobbies, like attending a car show or joining a civic club. Photo by Bruce Berg

(Right) One event looked forward to all year long is the Fourth of July parade, hosted annually by the city of Springfield. Photo by Bruce Berg

(LEFT) FERRIS WHEELS ARE A COUNTY FAIR STAPLE, AND LANE COUNTY NEVER LETS ITS RESIDENTS DOWN, HOSTING A FAIR EVERY YEAR COMPLETE WITH MIDWAY GAMES AND RIDES. PHOTO BY BRUCE BERG

(BELOW) A HIGHLIGHT OF THE EUGENE CELEBRATION IS THE GRAND PARADE, WITH TRADITIONAL AND NON-TRADITIONAL ENTRIES LINED UP TO CELEBRATE CIVIC PRIDE AND INDIVIDUALISM. PHOTO BY CHARLENE SABINI

FESTIVALS ARE MORE THAN JUST FOOD AND CONCERTS; THERE ARE PLENTY OF ACTIVITIES TO ENTERTAIN EUGENEANS OF ANY AGE. PHOTO BY CHARLENE SABINI

(LEFT) EUGENE'S MILD CLIMATE ALLOWS FOR A VARIETY OF OUTDOOR ACTIVITIES, LIKE BICYCLING THROUGH THE WILLAMETTE PASS. PHOTO BY BRUCE BERG

(BELOW) THE BASALT COLUMNS AT SKINNER'S BUTTE ARE POPULAR FOR ROCK CLIMBING. PHOTO BY BRUCE BERG

(BELOW LEFT) PHOTO © CHRIS LUNESKI

A SHORT DRIVE FROM EUGENE, THE COASTAL CITY OF NEWPORT IS SURE TO BE A DAY-TRIP LOADED WITH FUN. THE OREGON COAST AQUARIUM, FORMER HOME OF KEIKO (PICTURED ABOVE), STAR OF *FREE WILLY*, IS THERE, ALONG WITH MILES OF BEACHES. PHOTO BY BRUCE BERG

Eugene and Springfield are a haven to artists and art lovers alike. Local talent can display their work on the murals in downtown Springfield, and there are plenty of art shows and museums for the entertainment and education of Eugene-Springfield citizens, young and old. Photos by Bruce Berg

THE UNIVERSITY OF OREGON MUSEUM OF ART FEATURES MOSAIC BRICKWORK IN THIS SERENE COURTYARD AND FISHPOND. PHOTO © CHRIS LUNESKI

# Chapter Six

# 6

## *Eugene's Neighbors*

The Heceta Head Lighthouse is an active beacon and one of 11 lighthouses along the Oregon coast.
Photo by Larry Geddis

HECETA HEAD LIGHTHOUSE PROTECTS SHIPS AND SAILORS FROM THE ROCKS THAT JUT OUT OF THE OCEAN AT DEVIL'S ELBOW. PHOTO BY BRUCE BERG

LANE COUNTY COVERS ABOUT 4,550 SQUARE MILES AND IS ABOUT 90 PERCENT FORESTLAND, BOTH PUBLIC AND PRIVATE. PHOTO BY BRUCE BERG

Eugene and Springfield are situated in a thoroughly impressive neighborhood: Lane County, Oregon. In this one county you find majestic mountains; rushing cold-water rivers; gentle lakes; deep, shadowy forests; long expanses of wild ocean beaches; quaint, honest farm villages; and vibrant modern cities.

Lane County is named for General Joseph Lane, Oregon's first territorial governor. The county covers about 4,550 square miles, roughly the size of Connecticut. At its widest, it stretches about 150 miles from the Cascade Mountains in the east to the Pacific Ocean in the west. About 90 percent of Lane County is forestland, both public and private. The population is about 325,000, with a human density of about 71 people per square mile.

Eugene is the county seat and government, cultural, business, and geographical center of Lane County. People from throughout the county regularly travel to Eugene for business and to shop, dine, and attend plays, concerts, and college sporting events. People from Eugene frequently journey around the county for recreation and a change of pace.

A tour of Lane County takes you from the clouds to sea level and across ever-changing landscapes. Traveling east to west, you first meet the great wall of the Cascade Mountains. Amid this ancient craggy range stand the Three Sisters, a trio of timeless snow-capped peaks. On clear days, all three are visible from Eugene. South Sister, at 10,358 feet above sea level, is the highest point in Lane County.

Some 50 miles southwest of the Three Sisters Wilderness Area, in the lush Cascade foothills, are the towns of Oakridge and Westfir. Once lumber company towns, Oakridge and Westfir are now jumping-off points and supply stations for high-mountain adventures. The area has become a hotbed of mountain biking, one of the fastest-growing outdoor activities in Oregon. Hundreds of miles of mountain trails test the skills of cyclists of all levels. Each July, Oakridge holds the Fat Tire Festival, a mountain-biking event that attracts the top riders from throughout the Northwest.

Just north of Westfir you discover the Office Bridge, one of 20 covered bridges in Lane County. Covered bridges were common throughout Oregon by the end of the 19th century. By 1915, a standard design—the truss-and-housing design—was adopted by the state. Built of sturdy Northwest timbers, Lane County's covered bridges include such features as open windows, laminated floors, and interior whitewashing.

Lane County boasts of more covered bridges than any other county west of the Appalachians. Most are listed on the National Register of Historical Places and most are open to automobile or foot traffic. The county owns and maintains most of the bridges, while a few are owned by private companies, including the Office Bridge in Westfir. The Office Bridge is the longest covered bridge in Oregon and one of only two bridges in Lane County painted red.

The oldest covered bridge in Lane County is the Mosby Bridge, 30 miles west of Westfir near the town of Cottage Grove on the floor of the long and narrow Willamette Valley. Cottage Grove is known as "the covered bridge capital of Lane County." Six spans grace the landscape within a short drive from the town, including Centennial Bridge, across from City Hall in downtown

Cottage Grove. This footbridge was built in 1987 to commemorate the 100th anniversary of the founding of Cottage Grove.

Cottage Grove, 20 miles south of Eugene, has preserved much of its colorful logging and mining past. The downtown area retains an old-fashioned charm and is listed in the National Register of Historical Places. Nearby in the Bohemia Mining District, where gold was discovered in 1863, you can try your luck at panning for gold. Cottage Grove recognizes its mining past each July with the Bohemia Mining Days Celebration. The festival includes gold panning, a rodeo, and a grand parade.

Just north of Cottage Grove along Interstate 5, the principal north-south thoroughfare of the West Coast, sits Creswell. This small farming community is a welcome rest stop along the interstate and home to the Creswell Historical Museum and the popular Emerald Valley Resort, a world-class 18-hole golf course. Creswell celebrates an old-fashioned 4th of July each year with a pancake breakfast, parade, games, and fireworks.

Continuing along I-5 through Eugene and Springfield, you arrive in Coburg. Once a thriving mill town, Coburg is now a peaceful village with many preserved historical homes and an abundance of antique shops.

Northwest of Coburg on Highway 99W, once the main north-south route through Oregon, lies the farming community of Junction City, 20 miles north of Eugene. Settled by Scandinavian immigrants in the late 19th century, Junction City maintains its Norse heritage. Storefronts and parks reflect a Scandinavian design. Each August, residents stage the renowned Scandinavian Festival, four days of Scandinavian food, crafts, costumes, and entertainment.

Junction City sits on the edge of wine country. The South Willamette Valley—which extends from Benton County, north of Lane County, to Douglas County to the south—is home to some 18 wineries and hundreds of acres of grape vines. The region's loamy soils and long, mild growing seasons are similar to some of the prime wine-producing areas of Europe. Pinot Gris, White Riesling, Pinot Noir, Chardonnay, and Gewurztraminer are among the noble grape varieties cultivated in the South Willamette Valley. Most wineries are open for tours and tastings.

Continuing your tour of Lane County, you next cruise south on Highway 99W to Highway 126, through Eugene and westward toward the Pacific Coast. About 15 miles west of Eugene are the small twin towns of Veneta and Elmira. Veneta and Elmira are also known as the gateways to the Coast Range. Beginning here, the landscape graduates from flat valley to rolling foothills to high-country rain forests.

At its widest, Lane County stretches about 150 miles from the Cascade Mountains in the east to the Pacific Ocean in the west. Photo by Bruce Berg

**There are three dozen parks in Lane County, offering opportunities for fun across the full range of landscapes. Photo by Steve Terrill**

In the Coast Range, on or near Highway 126, you discover Camp Lane, Linslaw Park, and Mapleton Park, three of Lane County's three dozen county parks. Lane County parks offer opportunities for fun across the full range of landscapes. Depending on the park, you can camp, picnic, hike, swim, raft, sail, fish, or ride horseback.

The parks are divided into three districts. The McKenzie-Willamette District, in the eastern mountainous territory of the county, includes 16 parks offering mountain hiking, whitewater rafting, and river fishing. The Fern Ridge District has four parks within 16 miles of Eugene. All four are on the Fern Ridge Reservoir, a man-made lake and one of the best sailing venues in North America. The Coast District contains 13 parks, including several day parks with boat ramps accessing rivers and the unrivaled Harbor Vista Campground, a camp site right on the Pacific Coast.

The mighty Pacific marks the western boundary of Lane County. Highway 126, the east-west route, runs into Highway 101, or the Coast Highway, the north-south route, in the coastal town of Florence about 50 miles west of Eugene.

Traveling south on Highway 101, a designated National Scenic Byway, you find the Oregon Dunes National Recreation Area. Here, sand dunes as high as 500 feet stretch along 47 miles of protected coastline. You can explore the dunes on foot, on horseback, or in a dune buggy.

Heading back north along Highway 101, you arrive in the charming community of Florence, a working fishing port and tourist mecca. In Old Town, you can visit restaurants, antique shops, boutiques, and galleries; take an educational cruise up the Siuslaw River on a sternwheeler boat; and watch fishermen unload their catch.

Florence is home to the Rhododendron Festival in May and the Chowder, Blues, and Brews Festival in September. A highlight of this gathering is the clam chowder contest. Restaurateurs from up and down the Oregon Coast offer up their clam chowder creations to a panel of expert judges—food critics, restaurant owners, master chefs, and the general public—for the coveted title of Best Chowder On The Coast.

Traveling north of Florence on Highway 101, you come across Washburne State Park with its easily accessible tide pools and sea wildlife. Farther along the highway are the Sea Lion Caves, the world's largest sea cave and home to hundreds of Stellar and California sea lions. For a small fee, you can enter the cave and view one of nature's true spectacles.

Around the bend, at the end of the tour—and at the end of the continent—you spot the glorious Heceta Head Lighthouse, the most photographed lighthouse in the United States. Heceta Head is an active beacon and one of 11 lighthouses along the Oregon Coast.

Below the lighthouse, overlooking the ocean, sits Heceta House, the stately Victorian-style residence of the old lighthouse keepers. Heceta House is now a picturesque three-bedroom bed and breakfast open to the public.

What else could you want? Lane County has it all. □

IN LANE COUNTY YOU CAN FIND MAJESTIC MOUNTAINS; RUSHING COLD-WATER RIVERS; GENTLE LAKES; DEEP, SHADOWY FORESTS; LONG EXPANSES OF WILD OCEAN BEACHES; QUAINT, HONEST FARM VILLAGES; AND VIBRANT, MODERN CITIES. PHOTO BY BRUCE BERG

*"Centrally located in Lane County, Eugene Airport is the gateway to the Southern Willamette Valley, offering easy access to the resources and opportunities of the region. It is the second busiest airport in the State of Oregon and the fifth largest airport in the Pacific Northwest which enables visitors to explore the surrounding beauty of the area from dramatic rivers to beautiful coasts. The Eugene Airport has strived throughout the years to best suit the regional needs of the community and showcase the quality of life Eugene has to offer."*

**DIANA BELL**
*Office Manager*
*Eugene Airport*

Lane County boasts of more covered bridges than any other county west of the Appalachians, and most are listed on the National Register of Historic Places and open to foot or automobile traffic. Photo by Larry Geddis

Sailing is a favorite hobby in Lane County's coastal cities, such as Florence. Photo by Bruce Berg

*"Making a difference in the community comes down to personal commitment, dedication, and plain old hard work. St. Vincent's helps thousands of homeless and low income people every year—whether its emergency services or affordable housing or jobs/training. But this outreach would not be possible without the generous support of the City of Eugene, other organizations, and the individuals who give of their resources and their spirits. Please consider this an invitation to roll up your sleeves and get involved!"*

**Terry McDonald**
*Executive Director*
*St. Vincent De Paul Society of Lane County, Inc.*

Florence is also the location of the Sea Lion Caves, the world's largest sea cave and home to hundreds of Stellar and California sea lions. Photo by Bruce Berg

Lane County's lakes, rivers, and coastline nourish the land and enhance the quality of life immeasurably for all residents. Photo © Chris Luneski

(LEFT) THE SOUTHERN WILLAMETTE VALLEY IS HOME TO SOME 18 WINERIES AND HUNDREDS OF ACRES OF GRAPE VINES, PRODUCING NOBLE GRAPE VARIETIES FOR WINES SUCH AS PINOT GRIS, WHITE RIESLING, PINOT NOIR, CHARDONNAY, AND GEWURZTRAMINER. PHOTO BY BRUCE BERG

(BELOW) THE AREA'S MANY LAKES, RIVERS, AND WATERWAYS PROVIDE RECREATION OPPORTUNITIES THROUGHOUT THE YEAR. PHOTO BY STEVE TERRILL

(OPPOSITE) DEEP, LUSH GREEN IS A COMMON COLOR IN THE AREA SURROUNDING EUGENE-SPRINGFIELD. PHOTO © CHRIS LUNESKI

(FOLLOWING PAGE) AMONG THE CASCADE MOUNTAIN RANGE STAND THE THREE SISTERS, A TRIO OF SNOW-CAPPED PEAKS. THE SOUTH SISTER, AT 10,358 FEET ABOVE SEA LEVEL, IS THE HIGHEST POINT IN LANE COUNTY. PHOTO BY LARRY GEDDIS

63-01

# Chapter Seven

# 7

## *Manufacturing & Distribution*



Once ruled almost exclusively by the lumber industry, Eugene is now home to a broad range of manufacturers, thanks to the city's efforts over the years to diversify the local economy.
Photo by John Duffey

# Sony Disc Manufacturing

When the average citizen thinks of the Sony brand name, several different images may come to mind. Some may recall the fact that Sony was one of the originators of the compact disc genre; others may be more in tune with the company's latest foray into the technological field—the PlayStation 2 game console. Regardless of how consumers worldwide perceive the corporation, the citizens of Springfield see it as not only one of the corporate giants in the world, but also a valuable friend and leader in the community.

Springfield's Sony Disc Manufacturing (SDM) plant reigns as part of the largest producer of pre-recorded optical discs in the world, serving the needs of the education, entertainment, and information industries with high-quality products and reliable services. These services include digital authoring, graphic design, mastering, replication, packaging, distribution, and fulfillment for audio CD, CD-ROM, PlayStation™ game discs, and Web-connected discs. The Springfield plant joins two other ISO-certified locations in America in Pitman, New Jersey and Terre Haute, Indiana.

Founded in 1995 after an extensive search through several different states spanning the West coast, Springfield was chosen as the locale that stood head and shoulders above the rest due to its educated workforce, superb quality of life, and infrastructure. Situated on a scenic 89-acre site that borders the McKenzie River, this state-of-the-art, 335,000-square-foot facility manufactures up to 12 million units each month. With the Springfield plant, Sony has been put in the position to better serve the retail and distribution centers in not only the mountain and western regions, but internationally as well, shipping products across the waters to ports in Asia among others.

Operators and technicians perform random quality checks outside the replication clean room at Sony Disc Manufacturing-Springfield.

Being the leader in the disc manufacturing marketplace allows Sony economies of scale that it can pass on to its customers that no other CD manufacturer can compete against, including the best deals on shipping and printing of the packaging component. These deals, coupled with the fact that Sony co-developed the patent for the compact disc technology nearly two decades ago and has Sony engineering on its side, gives it the leading edge as the premier service provider in its market.

One fact has remained unchanged over the years. The Sony Corporation fully understands that its customers have always been the backbone of its success. Because each of its customer's markets can be as unique as the products and services that each supplies, every project the plant takes on is designed to ensure that the customer gets exactly what they want by the designated time in which they need the product. Fulfilling its role as a full-service partner equally focused on its customer's business strategies, SDM's customers get the services that they require when choosing to work with the leader of pre-recorded digital media.

The SDM plant has enjoyed a fruitful and productive existence since the day the doors first swung open in 1995. The capacity has been expanded several times

Sony employees show local fourth graders how the math they are learning in school is used in the disc manufacturing process.

as new products and services have dictated its growth in both size and workforce.The plant currently employs 272 people and operates seven days a week. More than two thirds of those employees are citizens of the Eugene-Springfield area, which has helped give the local economy a substantial boost since the plant first came to town.

"It is Sony Disc Manufacturing-Springfield's goal to enhance and contribute to our community, following the example of our parent company," says Monica Shovlin, Director of Marketing. "Our current focus is on United Way and the non-profit social service agencies they support in Lane County, as well as local educational programs."

Over the last four years, Sony Disc Manufacturing has worked together with over 70 different non-profit agencies in Lane County, forming several partnerships with local social service agencies, programs that promote Arts/Entertainment, and programs that enhance education. Some of the partnerships that Sony has formed include work with the Children's Miracle Network, the Relief Nursery, Birth to Three, the HIV Alliance, the McKenzie-Willamette Foundation, the Muscular Dystrophy Association and the American Cancer Society's "Relay For Life". Sony Disc Manufacturing also encourages volunteerism through its support of community events such as the Eugene Celebration, the Springfield Filbert Festival, and the Oregon Asian Celebration.

LOCAL HIGH SCHOOL STUDENTS TOUR THE SPRINGFIELD MANUFACTURING FACILITY. A GROUP OF SONY EMPLOYEE VOLUNTEERS ACT AS PLANT TOUR GUIDES FOR COMMUNITY GROUPS ON A REGULAR BASIS.

The future for SDM finds it exploring the broadband era carefully. Not content to rest on its laurels as the leader in the CD manufacturing business, SDM would also like to reign supreme in the information delivery business. Recently, SDM has become heavily involved with digital authoring services, compiling research and facts that will help give the corporation the leading edge in the field. This way, as delivery media change, Sony will find itself just as competitive in the newer broadband era. Thus, Sony Disc Manufacturing is preparing itself and its work force to ensure a commanding edge in the 21st century.

When potential customers begin to weigh their options of why Sony Disc Manufacturing should be the recipient of their business over its competitors, the facts alone speak for themselves. There is absolutely no need to go elsewhere when the originators and leaders of the technology are available to turn your dreams into realities at affordable prices. □

# McDonald Candy Co.

"You ain't seen nothing yet"—Ronald Reagan.

When the span of a company's existence reaches eight decades, it's a safe assumption that business is good. And at McDonald Candy, business has never been better.

Founded in 1924 in Medford, Oregon, Weir McDonald relocated his business of selling tobacco products to Eugene in 1928. First on Olive Street and then relocating to 5th Street, McDonald met with a great deal of success early on in his venture. He soon expanded the business by incorporating the sales of candy, wine, beer, food, and fountain products along with the cigars and cigarettes and turned a corner in his profits. In 1959, he moved the company to a large warehouse on Broadway. Because of the name McDonald Candy Company, it led people to the assumption that McDonald manufactured candy which was never the case.

But he sure sold his share of confections. So much so that today McDonald Candy is one of the most well respected and revered names in Eugene businesses.

McDonald took on the assumed business name of McDonald Wholesale for the food division and Western Beverage Co. for the beverage side with over 11,000 different items offered by the entire company. Western Beverage Co. became the exclusive distributor for the Anheuser-Busch Company, delivering the company's products from just north of Salem to Eugene, and Medford. Newport Roseburg, Coos Bay to the California border.

One of the more fascinating facts about McDonald is that he still makes it a habit to come to work each day, Monday through Friday. Born in 1899, McDonald turned 103 in 2002 and is regarded as one of the more dynamic personalities in the McDonald Candy Corporation. His 200 employees in Eugene speak highly of the man and the genuine adoration for him is felt when speaking to any of them. He has a total of 340 employees within western Oregon.

For several decades, when McDonald wasn't busy with the corporation, he could be found on safari hunts, racking up a remarkable 140 trophies from around the world. Since his retirement from safaris, McDonald has donated all of his trophies to organizations and museums throughout the country including the Tucson Wildlife Museum in Tucson, Arizona, letting others share in the joys that brought so much pleasure to his life.

With a strong sense of quality and a loyalty to his customers, McDonald has passed these traits down to each of his employees who take great pride in working for the McDonald Candy Co. where it is not an option to have a good attitude—it's a requirement.

It is indeed rare that a business would change so little in eight decades like McDonald Candy has. But when the company makes a commitment to go out of its way to offer only the finest quality of products, there's no need to change when you already have the best. □

Hunter's done well using a lens

Eugene man shoots with cameras as often as guns

HUNTER

"The essence of vision"—Successories.

# Monaco Coach Corporation

In the world of recreational vehicles, one name stands towering above the rest: Coburg's own Monaco Coach Corporation.

Monaco is one of the world's leading producers of luxury recreational vehicles with a product line of 28 motorcoach models and seven models of towable RV's to offer its customers. Brand name recreational vehicles such as Monaco, Holiday Rambler, Beaver, Safari, Royale Coach, and McKenzie have been manufactured in Lane County since 1995, resulting in a solid employment base for the area. And with 2,000 employees, Monaco serves as the largest private employer in Lane County, giving the city of Coburg a major corporation which brings commerce into the local economy in the form of employees as well as service and delivery customers visiting the area.

The success of the Monaco Coach Corporation can be traced back to three major events in the company's evolution. The current management team came into play in 1987 and decided to pick one area of the RV industry to specialize in, picking the high-end Class A motorhome, thus becoming the world's largest producer of the item. Then, in 1996, Monaco purchased Holiday Rambler, which was twice the size of the Monaco Coach Corporation, and integrated it into the relatively lean company, making Monaco more powerful, increasing the purchasing power, distribution, and presence in the marketplace. Finally, in 2001 Monaco acquired the SMC Corporation, a staunch competitor of Monaco's for many years which served as another component in the propelling of the corporation to its leadership in the field today.

Over the years, Monaco has also seen its stronghold on the industry tighten with a series of 20-plus innovations that have drastically affected the world of recreational vehicles. Chief among those has been a chassis built specifically for diesel motor homes known as the Roadmaster. At the time of its inception, people in the industry were looking to outside suppliers in order to purchase their chassis. Today, the idea has been widely copied by others in the industry, but Monaco is still regarded as the pioneers of this innovative device.

Monaco's Signature Series motorhome is the company's flagship model.

Travel trailers such as the Holiday Rambler Aluma-Lite have broadened Monaco's product lineup.

One would think that successful business ventures and innovative ideas would be enough to make Monaco the success that it has become. But it's the treatment of its customers that has earned the corporation its solid reputation as a company that cares. Monaco believes that each sale of an RV comes in two halves. The first half of the job is giving the customer the best product on the market while the second half is making sure that the product works the way that was promised to the consumer. An RV is a large, complicated, and sophisticated purchase for most customers and the company makes a steadfast promise to help every customer receive the most from their purchase.

With a strong commitment to its customers combined with a dedication to providing the latest in technologies, Monaco Coach Corporation will prove to be a leader in its field for many decades to come. □

# CHAPTER EIGHT

# 8

## *High Technology*



EUGENE EMBRACES INNOVATION AND IS SUCCESSFULLY STEERING A PATH INTO THE TECHNOLOGIES OF TOMORROW TODAY.
PHOTO BY JOHN DUFFEY

# INOVEC, INC.

INOVEC'S TECHNOLOGY INCREASES ACCURACY AND EFFICIENCY, AND REDUCES THE NUMBER OF LOGS IT TAKES TO MEET DEMAND FOR LUMBER PRODUCTS.

Throughout the years, Eugene has served as the home to generations of lumbermen who have earned their living working in the timber industry. For many decades it was the timber industry that propelled the city and fueled the local economy. Today, one local company stands proud as revolutionaries in the still-thriving industry with innovative and high-tech solutions to the challenge of lumber manufacturing.

Founded in Eugene in 1979, Inovec started from a need in the wood producing industry to achieve consistent lumber size accuracy. Before Inovec's computerized positioning technology became available, operators would merely eyeball a cut of wood and would have to rely on mechanical gears and chain mechanisms to move the wood to align it for the cut. This wasn't a problem in the early days when wood was relatively cheap and wasted wood wasn't seen as a detriment to the environment or operating costs. But as log prices increased, wood became more expensive, and at the same time, sawmills began feeling the squeeze of globalized lumber prices. Inovec foresaw a solution to this problem using technology to not only help size the lumber, but to help make better decisions about how to saw the logs to obtain the most value and yield. Today, Inovec is a leader in providing computerized lumber optimization systems to sawmills worldwide.

These "optimizers" are used to automate various processes of lumber manufacturing within the sawmills. They use precision laser sensors to measure the raw material, and then determine the most efficient and valuable cuts to make and control the machinery to make the cuts with an accuracy of a few thousandths of an inch. Each mill owner controls the variables, including product quality requirements and the relative values of grades and sizes of lumber based on the current market conditions. As a result, these optimizers have helped save a great deal of wood, typically recovering 10 percent to as much as 30 percent more lumber from each log than previous practices, while increasing product value and quality at the same time. Each of these systems increases volumetric recovery, grade recovery, sawing accuracy, and production volume without an increase in labor. In addition sawmills are able to control the priority of their various products to meet just-in-time market demands.

One of the most impressive facts is that Inovec's control systems save literally millions of board feet of logs each year due to the increased amounts of lumber recovered from each log. Inovec is proud of its role in contributing to the forest ecosystem health by assisting its customers to use our timber resources more efficiently.

While it is easy to assume that this automation might threaten the employment of mill workers, this has proven to

INOVEC'S STEREOSCAN™ FEATURES A THREE-DIMENSIONAL LASER SCANNER FOR OPTIMIZING THE SAWING OF LOGS.

INOVEC'S LASER SCANNER MEASURES THE SHAPE OF EACH PIECE SAWN FROM THE LOG.

not be the case. In most instances, Inovec's optimizers have taken the manual labor out of each job and put the operators in control of the computerized machines. Therefore, instead of replacing people, each system improves the working conditions of the people and enhances their safety in a potentially hazardous environment. By making mills more efficient and profitable, Inovec has helped preserve jobs in the timber industry, while doing its part to support the success of sustainable forest management.

Inovec currently employs over 50 people at its main office and production facility in Eugene and serves customers throughout the world. In this highly specialized field, expertise in the use and application of this technology is earned through experience and specialized training. This means that many of the company's technical employees travel worldwide, installing systems and instructing customers on the use of this new technology.

The worldwide lumber industry is a $75 billion industry, with half of that production occurring in North America. Inovec's focus and leadership is in the "Appearance Wood" market. Appearance wood includes both hardwood and softwood products where the visual appearance of the end product is important. These products are used in everything from structural members to high quality furniture and paneling.

Inovec performed over 650 installations in over 300 wood-producing locations to date, with over 80 percent of its customers in North America. Its customers include some of the largest producers, such as Weyerhaeuser and Georgia Pacific, as well as many of the smaller specialty companies like Zip-O Lumber in Eugene and Swanson Brothers in Noti. An increased focus on international sales has seen growth in Canada, New Zealand, South America, Australia, and Germany, with future opportunities expanding in Europe, and Russia.

As Inovec progresses into the 21st century, it has realized that the needs of its customers are driven by the changing needs of the end users of the lumber. As the company grows and learns how to better serve its customers, it will be focusing on what its customer's customers' needs will be. Inovec continues to expand its capabilities to serve its expanding global marketplace, producing high technology solutions for the industry that has shaped the Eugene-Springfield area for generations. □

INOVEC'S WANEMASTER™ SYSTEM CONTROLS THE EDGER—TYPICALLY PRODUCING 10 TO 15 PERCENT MORE VALUE THAN MANUAL EDGER SYSTEMS.

# Symantec

SYMANTEC OPENED ITS NEW, **200,000**-SQUARE-FOOT FACILITY IN LATE DECEMBER.

Nearly everyone who has ever owned a computer in the last two decades has used a product manufactured by Symantec. Founded in 1982, the company has become the world leader in Internet security according to the industry analyst firm Gartner Dataquest. Symantec provides a broad range of content and network security software and appliance solutions to individuals, enterprises, and service providers.

In order to make sure that these software programs and appliances operate smoothly, Symantec has several service centers located throughout the world including one in the Eugene/Springfield area. This facility houses customer service, technical support, order administration, and customer registration services for customers throughout North America.

Symantec originally came to the Eugene/Springfield area in 1993, after a yearlong evaluation of 19 potential sites. The company selected Eugene because of its standards for technical education, educational partnership opportunities, and overall quality of life and affordability.

SYMANTEC IS THE WORLD'S LEADING SECURITY SOFTWARE PROVIDER.

"When Symantec opened its facility in 1993, we had 120 employees on staff here," said Chris Monnette, senior director of global consumer services at Symantec. "At the time, we hoped to boost employment to 250 people. Little did we know that eight years later we would have close to 800 people working for us in the area." This dramatic growth prompted the company to find a new location to house its burgeoning workforce. At the end of last year, Symantec moved into a new, 200,000-square-foot building in Springfield.

Symantec's Springfield employees offer service and support to both home users and corporate customers. The company's primary means of providing technical support for consumers is through its award-winning service and support Web site. At this site, customers have access to more than 50,000 support documents. This is the same database that technical support and customer service agents use to answer questions over the telephone. This service is free and is available 24 hours a day.

Customers can also post technical questions for free on the Ask Symantec online discussion groups. The questions and answers posted to these discussion groups are available for public viewing. When a customer e-mails a question, it is automatically posted on the discussion group Web site. A technical support person then e-mails a response to the customer and posts the reply on the message board. These messages are searchable so that customers can see if anyone has already posted their particular question. Customers post an average of 15,000 messages per week to the English-language Ask Symantec discussion groups.

For those who want to pay for telephone support, live Queue Jockeys (QJs) greatly reduce the frustration customers experience while on hold. QJs play music, offer tech support tips, and update customers with live estimates of anticipated wait times. They even take song requests via e-mail.

It's plain to see that Symantec's service center has not only provided a large boost to the local economy since 1993, but has put the minds of Symantec users nationwide at ease as well. □

SYMANTEC HAS BEEN A MEMBER OF THE EUGENE/SPRINGFIELD COMMUNITY SINCE **1993**.

# PSC, Inc.

Every day, millions of people throughout the world are affected by the hard work and dedication of a local company which has played an integral part in the evolution of the retail industry. The company is PSC, Inc., a global provider of integrated data-collection products and services for retail supply chains. And its product that has revolutionized the retail industry is the point-of-sale bar code scanner.

Since 1974, PSC has continually been at the forefront of bar code scanners and their designs for high volume environments, installing over three million checkout scanners in supermarkets and retail outlets worldwide. Additionally, the corporation produces a series of products designed to collect data including mobile and wireless data-capture terminals, warehouse management software, self-checkout systems, and fixed-position and handheld bar code scanners which all help improve efficiency, speed, and agility in the retail and warehouse and distribution sectors. With a strong belief in a product's reliability as its most important feature, the 800 employees of PSC work diligently and strenuously to ensure each scanner's long product life through years of vigorous testing and simulated real-world stress. Pushing each product past its limitations allows the engineering team to gauge how it will perform once the product is on the market and at use in the stores.

PSC'S CORPORATE HEADQUARTERS RESIDE IN PORTLAND, OREGON.

The company's most recent innovative product is the Magellan™ 8500, the first and only scanner in the world equipped with the breakthrough SurroundScan™ 3D Scanning™ technology. Introduced in January of 2002, this "smart" scanner is able to effectively scan products for the bar code on all six sides of an object, significantly increasing productivity and even allowing the reading of poor quality and truncated labels on products. This new technology will aid in speeding up the process of getting in and out of a grocery or retail store with its 360 degree scanning of millions of products throughout the world. In addition, the Magellan 8500 performs with a power consumption of less than 14 watts which could in turn can save a store up to 42 percent on its current electricity costs as compared to competitive scanners.

With a strong focus on consumers, PSC takes a great deal of pride in its dealings with customers. Understanding that the point of sale in retail and grocery stores can result in a bottleneck for the retail supply chain, PSC strives each day to create better solutions in order to speed this important part of the shopping experience that in the end benefits everyone involved.

Serving as a true leader in its industry, PSC, Inc. has truly made an impact on everyday life for the entire planet and will continue to do so as technology continues to flourish. □

PSC'S RESEARCH, DEVELOPMENT, AND MANUFACTURING FACILITY IN EUGENE.

TELELECT
SIMON-TELELECT

# CHAPTER NINE

# 9

## *Transportation, Energy & Natural Resources*



WHETHER THEY'RE INDIVIDUALS, BUSINESSES, SCHOOLS, OR ORGANIZATIONS, ALL RESIDENTS OF EUGENE RELY ON THE CITY'S INFRASTRUCTURE OF ENERGY, TRANSPORTATION, AND NATURAL RESOURCES TO MAINTAIN THE HEALTHY PULSE OF LOCAL LIFE. PHOTO BY CHARLENE SABINI

# Eugene Airport

**Eugene Airport serves as a gateway to the southern Williamette Valley.**

It was 1919 when local businessman and chairman of the Eugene Chamber of Commerce Aviation Committee Mahlon Sweet persuaded the people of Eugene to assist him in the establishment of the Eugene Air Park, Eugene's first municipal airport and the first municipally owned airport on the West Coast. Airplane rides were offered at the steep price of $15 for 15 minutes of sailing into the wild blue yonder. Even at those hefty price tags, the Air Park found curious thrill-seekers lining up for their chance to tour the skies in the amazing flying machines.

By 1939, Sweet had successfully campaigned to have a larger, more modern airport constructed for the city of Eugene. The city purchased land west of Highway 99 and on May 1, 1943, Mahlon Sweet Field was dedicated as 8,500 spectators flocked to the new airport on a day declared as Eugene Aviation Day. Eugene's first lady, Mrs. Elisha Large was on hand to christen the first commercial airline that landed at the airport with a bottle of champagne, signifying the beginning of a new era for Eugene.

Today, Mahlon Sweet Field, now known as the Eugene Airport, is the second busiest airport in the State of Oregon and the fifth largest airport in the Pacific Northwest. The Airport has been classified as a primary commercial service small hub airport, supporting both commercial flights and general aviation activity, serving approximately 750,000 passengers each year. The Airport serves a six-county region in mid-Oregon with 24 commercial arrivals and departures each day. Along with safety and security, its primary goal is to maintain and improve airline service for residents in the area, managing to succeed at this through airlines such as America West Express, Horizon, United, and United Express providing commercial connections to all parts of the nation and the world every day with direct non-stop service to many western cities.

A large factor in the successful growth of the airport can be attributed to the partnership with the Eugene Chamber of Commerce that resulted in the development of a "travel bank" in 1999. The "travel bank" is a depository of funds collected from 50 local companies to lure new air service to the community and has met with wonderful results. As part of this agreement, Horizon Air and American West Airlines signed on to provide direct non-stop flights to cities not previously served from Eugene. And while the commercial aspect of the airport keeps growing each

**Eugene Chamber of Commerce and Eugene Airport discuss air service needs with airline officials.**

year, the general aviation business has also thrived since the airport's relocation in 1956. Today, there are over 180 general aviation aircraft based at Mahlon Sweet Field, including many corporate aircraft owned by local area businesses that rely heavily on the air transportation system.

The airport is also home to one full service and two limited fixed base operators that provide general aviation services such as aircraft fueling and maintenance. In the 1990s, hangar construction increased dramatically at the airport, eventually occupying all of the space originally allotted for the venture.

Recent renovations have also assisted in the Eugene Airport's success. A $20 million landside expansion project that the public heavily invested in was completed in 1990. Between 2000 and 2002, terminal upgrades were completed to better provide for passenger needs. Some of these improvements included the modernization of the upper concourse deli and full-service restaurant and the construction of covered stairways and a covered walkway that allows passengers to board regional aircraft, remaining safe and dry no matter what the weather. These projects are just some of the examples of the airport's commitment to meet the needs of its customers, providing ease and convenience when they use the Airport.

THE B-GATE COVERED WALKWAY PROVIDES A SAFE, COMFORTABLE BOARDING EXPERIENCE FOR REGIONAL AIRLINE CUSTOMERS.

There are additional plans in effect to develop other facets of the airport, including expanding the airfield in order to provide a parallel runway. This additional runway will improve safety and capacity, and help broaden the services already offered at the Airport. Future plans include the expansion of the terminal building to include additional concessions and holding rooms with additional seating. The Airport's parking lot will be expanded to accommodate demand; a new entrance and internal circulation roads are being planned as well as an expansion of the general aviation area for additional hangar buildings. These changes will take place soon in order to accommodate increasing traffic and to provide exceptional service to the region.

The Eugene Airport has strived throughout the years to best suit the regional needs of the community and showcase the quality of life Eugene has to offer. The metamorphosis of the once small rural operation into a more sophisticated full-service commercial and general aviation facility has proven to be one of the most significant advances in Eugene's history and will continue to be a barometer on which the success of the city will be measured. □

WINGS, A CONTEMPORARY AIRPORT EATERY, OFFERS CUSTOMERS A UNIQUE SELECTION OF NORTHWEST FOOD AND WINE.

# GIUSTINA FAMILY

The timber industry has always played an integral part in the history of Eugene. While there have been many casualties in the local timber business, one name has persevered and continues to thrive today—Giustina—which has spawned three generations of timber management.

The Giustina brothers first came to America from Northern Italy in the early 1900s to forge a better life for themselves in the land of freedom and opportunity. After working as carpenters from New York to Portland, Oregon, the brothers decided to enter the forest products business in 1917 and bought a small sawmill in Molalla, Oregon.

In 1923, they moved their families to Lane County and purchased a sawmill east of Eugene in the Lost Creek Valley on Gossage Creek. In Lane County, the Giustina brothers "dug in their roots"and the original millsite and timberlands, logged in the 20s and 30s, are still owned by the family today as part of their managed forest.

In 1941, the Lost Creek mill was dismantled and the Giustinas built a new modern sawmill in Eugene at Second Avenue and Garfield Street. The new mill included a steam-generated electric plant, which sold electricity to the Eugene Water and Electric Board during non-peak hours. The second generation of Giustinas was now running the operation and a new era had begun.

During World War II, the mill produced and shipped Douglas fir products for the building of Army camps, mine sweepers, landing craft, and aircraft carrier decks. Following the war, the Giustinas helped the nation meet the demands for wood products and they continued to expand their operations, purchasing more timberland and expanding their operations with a veneer plant in 1952 and a plywood plant in 1959.

Beginning in the 1960s, competition was intense, government regulations increased, and consolidations within the industry began. Eugene was also growing and an expanding population was not as tolerant of the dust and noise of an industrial operation as it once had been. Wilderness legislation soon followed along with the environmental pressures that restricted the forest management activities on public (U.S. Forest Service and Bureau of Land Management) forestlands.

In 1988, the last of the mill operations were shut down and the third generation of Giustinas turned their attention to what they knew best—timberland management. In 1990, the Giustinas divided into three timberland management companies—Giustina Land and Timber Co., Giustina Resources, and Giustina Woodlands.

The Giustina family, in 1944, had one of the first nationally certified "tree farms" in Oregon. Today, the family continues their stewardship as they intensively manage their lands on a sustainable basis. Trees are the family's future—the forestland is a long-term investment that is nurtured and, following harvest, the land is planted again immediately with site-specific tree seedings.

To remain competitive in today's global marketplace, all segments of the forest products industry have modernized. Silvicultural research and technology have helped to maintain the Pacific Northwest as the world's forestry leader. Today foresters are highly educated professionals who mix technical knowledge with on-the-ground, site-specific, practical experience, utilizing hand-held computers and global positioning systems to assist them.

The private forestlands of Lane County make a vital contribution to the Eugene area by providing jobs, products, a tax base, and other social and economic benefits. Well-managed forests are sustainable and enhance forest resources—timber, water, fish and wildlife, soil, air, and scenic resources—well into the future.

The Giustina family is supportive of Oregon's forest protection laws and the Oregon Plan for Salmon and Watersheds. In 1971, the "Oregon Forest Practices Act" became the first legislation of its kind in the nation to govern forest management and harvest activities. Overseen and enforced by the Oregon Department of Forestry, the Act has been modified and expanded in response to new information and changing social, economic, and ecological needs. Citizens of Oregon can be proud of the laws Oregon has enacted to protect its forests.

As the Giustinas enter the 21st century, they are understandably proud of the family's heritage and dedication to being active members of the community. With the three companies all having deep roots in the area, business decisions are often made with the heart rather than solely on financial strategies. The Giustinas strive to provide a sustainable income for their families while providing stable employment for their employees and contractors. It is that family dedication that goes back to their grandfathers that keeps the Giustinas working hard and investing in not just the future generations of Giustinas, but also the future of the city of Eugene. □

# Home Comfort Heating & Air Conditioning, Inc.

When starting a business, there's no better business partner than a family member. So it was only natural that Wally Elling called upon his two sons Jeff and Dave to help him launch Home Comfort Heating and Air Conditioning, Inc. in 1992. Years later, the business has grown from three employees to over 50 employees and is regarded as one of the top Carrier and LENNOX dealers in the Northwest.

The company has a diversified clientele, servicing residential, commercial, industrial sites, and more. Known as Lane County's Energy Experts, Home Comfort's goal is to professionally evaluate each customer's needs and provide them with a workable solution that will meet or exceed any expectations while offering a fair and competitive price. Throughout its history, Home Comfort has grown primarily through referrals from satisfied customers, which has earned the company a solid reputation amongst the people of Eugene. The company continues to service all of its customers with the same enthusiastic energy and commitment that it takes to keep its position as one of Lane County's true leaders in the heating and air conditioning field.

The staff at Home Comfort have a sincere desire to develop and engineer new ways to make their customers' lives at home or their business more comfortable. The company stands firmly behind innovative alternative energy systems such as solar heating, geo-thermal systems, and zoning systems. A Zoning system allows you to customize your indoor weather according to the demands of your home and lifestyle. Each room has its own thermostat, giving you individual temperature control of each space. Geo-thermal systems are one of the most efficient heating and cooling systems available. Using the earth's endless supply of free energy, it operates at the fraction of the cost of conventional systems. A by-product of the heating and cooling process of a geothermal system provides free domestic water heating to your home resulting in substantial energy savings.

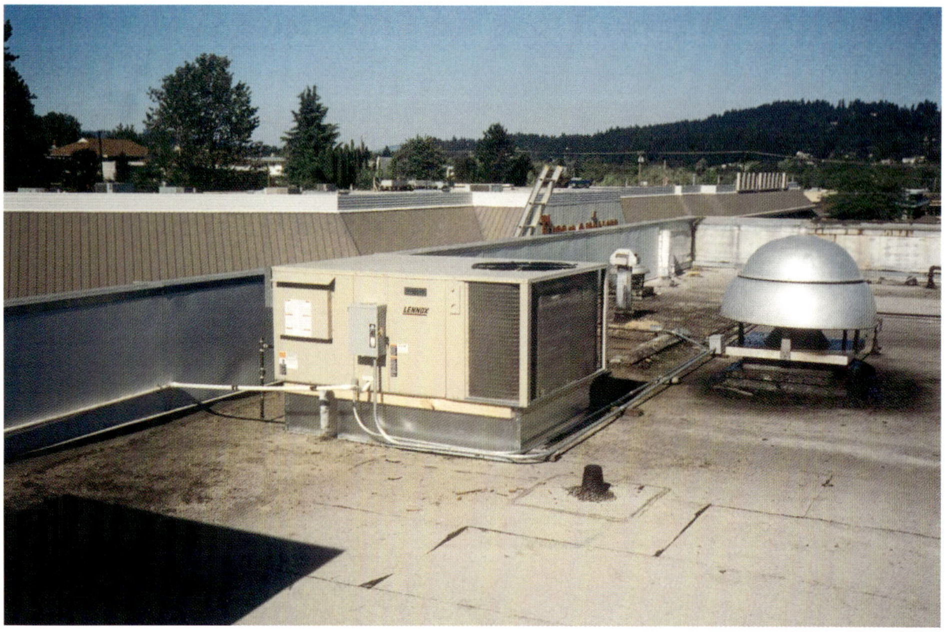

THE COMPANY HAS A DIVERSIFIED CLIENTELE—SERVICING RESIDENTIAL, COMMERCIAL, INDUSTRIAL SITES, AND MORE.

In addition, Home Comfort utilizes its own sheet metal fabrication shop for all of its work. The shop allows its staff to design and fabricate all ductwork and fittings in-house, using copper, stainless steel, and sheet metal.

FOUNDING OWNERS, LEFT TO RIGHT, JEFF ELLING, WALLY ELLING, AND DAVE ELLING.

Home Comfort features Carrier and LENNOX heating and cooling products, regarded as the leading manufactures in the heating and cooling industry.

The future for Home Comfort will find it growing in the commercial installation, service, and controls market. Home Comfort is working and partnering with Carrier in exploring alternative energy use such as fuel cells. The company realizes that fuel cells will most likely prevail as the leading alternative fuel source in the next ten years. Home Comfort and Carrier are working towards implementing this technology.

The Home Comfort name has become synonymous with quality in Eugene. "Our reputation is built on satisfied customers," says owner Jeff Elling. The Ellings and their staff are proud of the company's heritage and hope their customers feel they are a dealer that can be counted on for years to come. □

PHOTO BY BRUCE BERG

## Chapter Ten

# 10

## *Business & Finance*



**Knowledge and the capital to make business happen—that's the role of Eugene's business and finance organizations. Photo by Charlene Sabini**

# The Eugene Area Chamber of Commerce

The Eugene Area Chamber of Commerce has been part of the community since 1902, helping promote a healthy climate for business, and working to maintain the quality of life that makes the area such an attractive place in which to live and work.

A century ago, the organization was small. But now, just as the community has grown and matured, so too has the Chamber. Today, its 1,250 Chamber members represent a broad spectrum of businesses and service organizations. Big and small, these organizations help lead the way in promoting and maintaining the community's vitality.

Some of these Chamber members have been around even longer than the Chamber itself. Just as has happened to the Chamber, these "elder" businesses too have grown and changed with the times. But along the way, they provide a continuity that has brought the Eugene area from the past, and now helps it aim toward the future.

THE EUGENE CHAMBER BUILDING, EXPANDED AND REMODELED IN 1999, SERVES AS HEADQUARTERS FOR FIVE BUSINESS AND ECONOMIC DEVELOPMENT ORGANIZATIONS MAKING IT A ONE-STOP LOCATION FOR BUSINESS ASSISTANCE.

It is through the current efforts of these Chamber members and others that the groundwork is laid for a healthy future.

Today, the Chamber's job is to:

- Promote the success of the small businesses that make up the bulk of the economic demographics and its membership.
- Work to ensure that public policy decisions at the local level are made in the best interest of the economic and social well-being of the area.
- Assure that community development plans are implemented in a way that assures a healthy community, long into the future.

The Chamber carries out its mandate through the efforts of a number of committees, and a variety of events and functions. And, since it is a membership-driven organization, what the Chamber can accomplish is only done through the hard work and commitment of those members who volunteer their time, energy, and expertise.

Along with the committees that are set up to work on public policy and other business issues, the Chamber does its work through such programs as Business After Hours, Business-To-Business trade shows, golf tournaments, and job fairs. Through these and other events, the Chamber provides networking opportunities for our members to connect with each other, and thus help them grow their own businesses.

The growth of existing and new businesses is supported through seminars, workshops, problem solving, and other programs.

Through these and other efforts, the Chamber has been able to achieve a variety of successes.

One of the Chamber's most successful ventures took place in 1998 when they realized a long-standing vision of providing the business community with a one-stop shop for business assistance. After successfully conducting a $1.1 million capital campaign, the Chamber was able to build a new headquarters that not only houses the Chamber, but also four other business and economic development entities that serve the metropolitan area.

Another recent success has been the innovative, nationally recognized program for air service recruitment. By developing a "travel bank" the Chamber partnered with

DURING THE 1800S THE MILL RACE WAS HOME TO GRISTMILLS AND SAWMILLS. PHOTO COURTESY OF SALLY McALEER, CONVENTION & VISITORS ASSOCIATION OF LANE COUNTY OREGON

the city of Eugene and the Eugene Airport to launch an aggressive campaign to add commercial air service at the airport.

In sum, the Chamber's job is to create an environment in which businesses can be successful, so that the strength of the area's economy matches and contributes to the quality of life in Eugene.

It has been a changing landscape. As the timber industry became a less important factor in the economic picture, the Chamber has worked to bring in other businesses more in tune with the business climate of the times.

The Chamber has helped to achieve this by working to draw new business and industries to the area, including the relocation and expansion of a number of technology based companies, as well as several Fortune 500 companies.

Such industry leaders as Sony Disc Manufacturing, Symantec, Levi Strauss, and subsidiaries of GMC have all become substantial members of the local economy, providing the city and its inhabitants with a wealth of jobs and opportunities.

Along with its healthy local economy, Eugene also takes pride in a national reputation for the quality of life that is to be found. The city of Eugene has appeared on several lists of the best places in America to live, usually near the top of these lists. The cable television network A&E featured a series of the ten cities in America that "have it all" and Eugene appeared on that list as well. Eugene has also been listed in several publications as one of the top mid-sized cities in which to retire as well as one of the top ten college towns in the West.

The Chamber's job is to help nourish and maintain the economic climate in the community, so that during the next hundred years, residents are able to maintain what their community has brought from the past, and made it what it is today.

The Chamber is only able to sustain this effort through the support and dedication of its members, and of the community that has provided the framework in which so much has been accomplished, and where there is so much more to be done to lead the Eugene area into a secure, prosperous future. □

HENDRICKS PARK, EUGENE'S FIRST CITY PARK, HAS 77 ACRES OF FORESTED PARK LAND AND CONTAINS OVER FIVE THOUSAND RHODODENDRONS AND OTHER ORNAMENTAL PLANTS. PHOTO COURTESY OF SALLY MCALEER, CONVENTION & VISITORS ASSOCIATION OF LANE COUNTY OREGON

# Centennial Bank

Centennial Bank is an independent, locally owned and managed commercial bank. Centennial Bank is publicly traded (Nasdaq: CEBC) and listed on the Russell 2000 Index. As an Oregon-based bank, serving customers from 16 full-service branch locations along the I-5 corridor between Vancouver, Washington, and Cottage Grove. Centennial Bancorp and Centennial Bank have headquarters in Portland, while Eugene serves as the bank's central administrative hub, and is home to the Real Estate Division.

Besides branches, the bank operates seven Commercial Banking Centers to provide relationship-based financial services to middle-market business clients. Centennial's Real Estate Division—Centennial Mortgage—has an additional four offices based in Eugene and Portland. Centennial Bank also caters to retirees, managing seven branches exclusively in Portland area retirement centers.

**The bank's administrative center is located in downtown Eugene.**

**Centennial Bank has a long history of service and community involvement throughout the Eugene/Springfield area and Lane County.**

Whatever the venue, Centennial emphasizes superior customer service at every level to commercial and industrial clients, business enterprises, public entities, professionals, executives, and individuals. The bank provides customers with a broad suite of business and consumer financial products, including new offerings such as CB-Onlinebanking, Online Bill Pay, business insurance alliances, and Merchant Banking. Centennial Mortgage complements the bank with a full range of residential mortgage and commercial real estate lending products.

Centennial Bancorp has demonstrated an impressive financial track record since it was established in 1981, ranking among the most profitable banking organizations in the western region of the country. As of December 31, 2001, Centennial Bancorp assets stood at $815 million, more than double since 1996.

Centennial's success is due, in part, to its unique approach with business clients. Centennial's experienced executive management team, headed by 30-year industry veteran President and Chief Executive Officer Ted R. Winnowski, places a special emphasis on "high touch and right touch" personal service. Not unlike the days when doctors made house calls, Centennial's highly motivated and seasoned bank officers from the top down frequently call directly on the businesses they serve. This direct, personalized approach facilitates a true understanding of customer needs to tailor right-fitting and integrated financial service solutions.

The ever-increasing list of offerings includes professional accounts, executive accounts, ultra rate fund accounts, cash management services, equipment leasing, merchant bankcard services, and tiered money market accounts. Increasingly, Centennial is partnering with other companies to provide customers with even more product options. Its latest online service, for example, provides small business employers, consisting of two to 50 employees, with flexible and convenient options for purchasing name-brand, affordable employee benefit insurance products.

"We believe our success rests with our ability to understand our customers' needs and support their success," Winnowski said.

Centennial Bank's commitment to the community extends well beyond business and personal banking service to the most personal level. Since many of organization's employees have lived and worked in their respective communities for years, they are well known figures with strong attachments to community activities. Officers make significant contributions through regular civic involvement and participation.

CEO Winnowski points with pride to these employees when he says, "Our exceptional employees characterize our mission: that we persistently strive for excellence and superior performance in our organization—and at Centennial Bank we are always "Open for business—everywhere we do business!" □

*Member FDIC. Equal Housing Lender.*

PHOTO BY LARRY GEDDIS

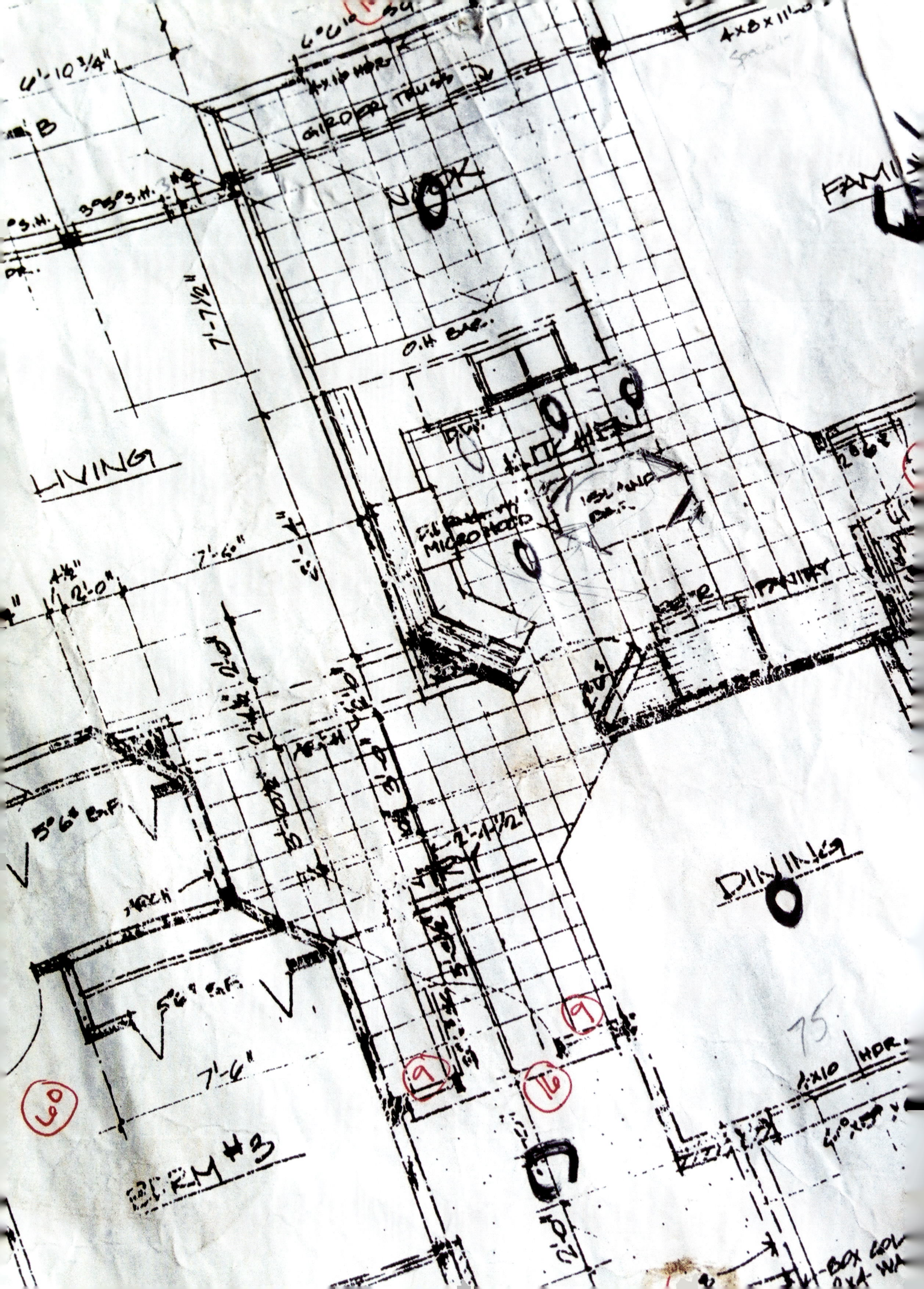
GIRDER TRUSS
NOOK
O.H. CAB.
LIVING
KITCHEN
ISLAND BAR
MICROHOOD
PANTRY
DINING
BDRM #3
4'-10 3/4"
7'-7 1/2"
7'-6"
2'-0"
7'-6"
5'6" B.F.
4x10 HDR.

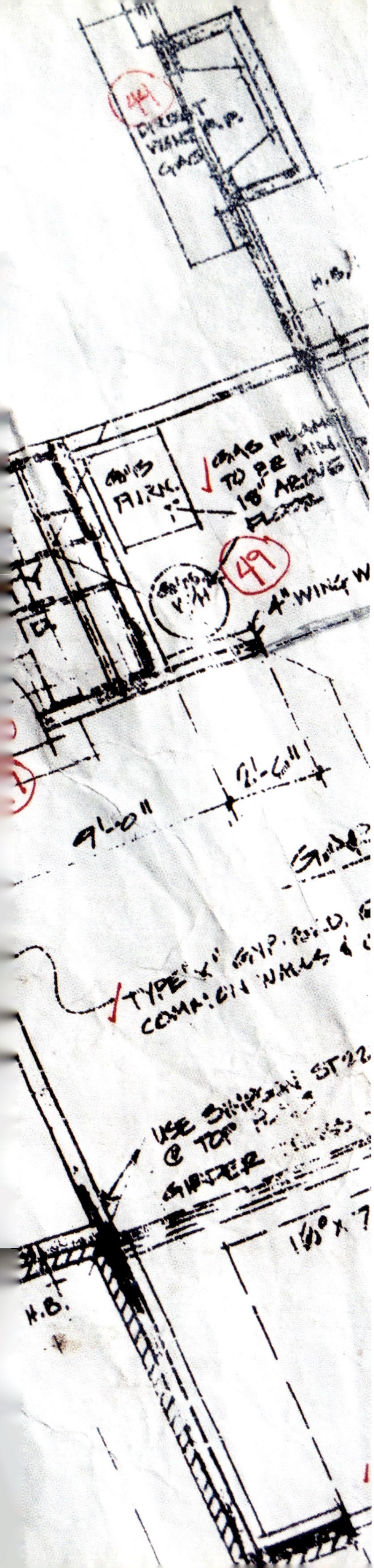

# Chapter Eleven

## 11

## *Real Estate, Development & Construction*



Keeping pace with the city's commercial and residential growth is the challenge of Eugene's real estate and development experts. Photo by Charlene Sabini

# St. Vincent de Paul Society of Lane County, Inc.

GRAND OPENING OF AFFORDABLE HOUSING.

Mark Twain said: "When the only tool you have is a hammer, all your problems start looking like nails."

St. Vincent de Paul Society of Lane County, Inc. (SVDP) has been hammering out solutions to poverty and homelessness since 1954. The society of St. Vincent de Paul was founded in France in 1833 by Frederick Ozanam, a college student challenged to put his Christian ideals into practice in every day life. His example has captured the imagination of volunteers around the world. Ozanam chose St. Vincent de Paul, a 16th century saint known for his love of the poor, as the patron for the Society, which was first established in the United States in St. Louis, Missouri.

Eugene faces the complex social problems common to all communities of this size: homelessness, hunger, scarcity of affordable housing, and the need for new jobs. SVDP, with the help of thousands of volunteers, cooperation among other non-profits, and the support of local government, has responded in creative ways.

### SUSTAINABLE WASTE-BASED BUSINESS OR HOW TO TURN A DONATED REFRIGERATOR (CAR, CLOTHING, BOOKS, COMPUTERS, WOOD, ETC.) INTO JOBS, TRAINING, AFFORDABLE HOUSING, AND EMERGENCY SERVICES

St. Vincent de Paul's Thrift Stores provide important revenue and goods for the Agency's charitable programs. But "Vinnie's" has transcended the typical re-sale clothing and donated furniture product mix to include a variety of sustainable waste-based businesses thereby creating jobs and opportunities. Whether it is repairing and recycling appliances or mattresses, building furniture, recycling computers, or creating architectural and gift items from discarded window pane glass, St. Vincent de Paul is dedicated to a responsible re-use of resources, adding value to items that would otherwise go into overflowing landfills. These recycle/re-use businesses create hundreds of jobs and training opportunities, while generating funding for affordable housing and emergency services. St. Vincent's model is receiving national recognition.

EUGENE MAYOR JIM TORREY WITH FUTURE BASEBALL STARS FROM *VINNIE'S KIDS*.

### SELF-SUFFICIENCY: LEARNING TO MAKE IT ON YOUR OWN

"Why don't they just get a job?" is a question often asked regarding the people standing on street corners with cardboard signs. St. Vincent de Paul's self-sufficiency programs help people learn the skills they need to gain and keep a job. A variety of vocational service and training programs help youth and adults help themselves to a better, more productive life. Educational programs such as Second Chance Renters Rehabilitation teach people their rights and responsibilities as renters and help them gain stable housing.

### BUILDING HOUSING, BUILDING COMMUNITY

Home ownership is part of the American dream—and that dream can come true for low income households in the community. St. Vincent de Paul is the largest non-profit developer of affordable housing in Western Oregon. Housing ranges from permanent, affordable rentals and transitional housing with case management, to home ownership opportunities. Well-established partnerships with Shelter Care, Birth to Three, ARC of Lane County, and many others ensure housing success for specialized populations. St. Vincent's housing is an asset to any neighborhood—it's beautiful, safe, well-built, with attractive design and energy saving features.

The heart of St. Vincent de Paul's Aurora Glass foundry.

Building affordable housing is important, but it takes more than 4 walls and a roof. An extensive Resident Services Program helps tenants organize each complex, and coordinates enrichment classes, including the Threshold Home Ownership Program. Hundreds of resident children are reached through children's programs, a Vinnie's Kids sports team, and specialized clubs for formerly homeless youth. Building families and strengthening neighbors results in a stronger community.

### HELPING HANDS

Making a difference in the community comes down to personal commitment, dedication, and plain old hard work. SVDP's Social Service Office volunteer staff coordinates thousands of calls for help and the response of dedicated teams of volunteers. Outreach includes energy/rental assistance, clothing, prescription medicines, emergency transportation, beds, and school supplies. Over 50 faith communities, with thousands of volunteers, care for homeless families through the Interfaith Emergency Shelter System. First Place Family Center offers day services to homeless families with children including a state-certified child care center, after school club for older children, laundry/shower facilities, food, clothing, and emergency services. With the help of the City of Eugene, local businesses provide safe, legal parking places for homeless people living in their cars. An outreach worker helps each person plan for a permanent housing solution. Another innovative housing program pairs home owners with homeless people who work out a shared housing arrangement. Hunger is an issue in the community. Over 1,000 food boxes are given away each month to hungry families while homeless single people can access food and other services at the Eugene Service Station. St. Vincent's outreach would not be possible without the generous support of the City of Eugene, other organizations, and the individuals who give of their resources and their spirits. Please consider this an invitation to roll up your sleeves and get involved!

Preserving our natural environment, creating a community environment where people are fed, clothed, housed, and given the opportunity to help themselves: this is the work of St. Vincent de Paul Society of Lane County, Inc. □

Woodshop staff member making a bookcase.

Arlie & Company salutes St. Vincent de Paul and is proud to underwrite this profile.

# McKay Investments Company, LLC

While everyone in Eugene knows Oakway Center for its wealth of shopping opportunities, at least two people in the city remember when a family farm stood there amongst the mighty Oak trees. That's because the farm belonged to their grandparents and today those two siblings, Doug McKay and Linda McKay Korth, are the second generation proprietors of McKay Investments which not only manages Oakway Center, but keeps the McKay family tradition alive in the middle of a bustling business district.

**Oakway Center offers a diverse mix of fine shopping for the entire family.**

Developed in the mid to late 60s, Oakway Center is celebrating its recent redevelopment with a whole new look. A cozy yet spacious courtyard built adjacent to the Oakway Center is surrounded by popular eating establishments and unique shops attracting customers from all over the area. A stage is nestled in one corner of the courtyard with live entertainment available making this not just a shopping center, but a lifestyle center, one that can be used equally for shopping as well as such events as wedding receptions and family reunions. Still, with all this new growth, the McKays insisted that the trees in the new courtyard which once stood between the old family homestead and the barn remained, serving as landmarks of their heritage. Once inside the courtyard, a keen eye will discover that one of the buildings has an indention built into it in order to aid in protecting the roots of the tree standing directly in front of the shop. While at the front of Oakway Center stands an 80-foot tall tree that is decorated each holiday season and billed as the largest Christmas Tree south of Portland. It's the same tree that the McKay's grandmother used to sit under and sell peaches on the side of Coburg Road when the road was a two lane county road. When it comes to preserving family tradition, the McKays go to great lengths to make sure the past isn't soon forgotten.

On the backside of Oakway Center resides five office buildings which are also owned and managed by McKay Investments. These buildings were placed strategically to protect the neighborhood to the north away from the bright lights and traffic that emanate from Oakway Center. Other locations owned and managed by McKay Investments include the West 11th Shopping Center, the Mohawk Shopping Center, and Springfield Mall as well as several industrial warehouses in the Eugene-Springfield area.

Doug and Linda share ownership of the company with their five respective children and are planning to pass their ownership in McKay Investments down to their grandchildren soon. Which is a fitting act as they will be placing the same level of trust in their 11 grandchildren to keep the family tradition alive as their parents once placed in them. □

**McKay Investment company's flagship property is the Oakway Center. The center is situated on 25 acres located at the corner of Oakway and Coburg Roads in the heart of Eugene's Ferry Street Bridge area.**

# Builder's Electric

When Builder's Electric was first established in 1960, its humble beginnings consisted of two electricians and two trucks providing the best possible service to the city of Eugene.

It's safe to report that quite a lot has changed since the early days of the business. The amount of employees has grown from two to a whopping 65 employees driving a team of 45 trucks, each employee dedicated to providing the best electrical service for the lowest rate possible in the city. No job is too big for Builder's Electric, be it commercial, residential, or industrial work. Each employee is trained and experienced in every type of labor that may be required to complete an assignment. Licensed, bonded, and insured, at Builder's Electric service is more than just courtesy, competitive rates, and fast and efficient service. It's the ability to offer the customer such amenities as radio dispatch service for fast responses to the customer's needs, troubleshooting, bucket truck services, load surveys, and much more.

**Chambers Media Center.**

**US Bank Tower, Downtown Eugene.**

Fred Wittkop, President of the electrical contracting firm, bought the business in 1974 and has turned it into one of the major forces in its field in the Eugene area. Wittkop worked for the General Electric Company for several years and was transferred to Eugene, a city in which he and his wife Peggy fell in love with instantly. Working as an engineer, Wittkop found himself working on a project and could not find an electrical contractor who grasped just what he was trying to do. After expressing his concern with Peggy, she suggested that he find a way to tackle the project himself. This is all the push he needed to purchase Builder's Electric and build it into the success story that it is today.

Wittkop admits that his business has been truly blessed to work with some of the more influential businesses in Eugene including the Grain Mill, Giustina Land and Timber, Monaco Coach Corp., Peace Health, PSC Inc., Symantec Corp., and Twin Rivers Plumbing. In addition to the good fortunes that the company has had working in conjunction with various corporations, Wittkop is quite proud of his team of employees, many of whom began their careers serving as apprentices through a state-sponsored program and have never left the business after finishing their apprenticeship. Wittkop finds that once the apprentices have finished the four-year program they fully understand what's expected of them and are already familiar with the work involved in making the company one of the finest in its field.

Builder's Electric has grown and prospered since it first opened for business and will continue to do so in the future with daughter Kelly O'Brien and son-in-law Darrin Lajoie willing to assume second generation ownership. Meeting the customer's needs and striving to fulfill all expectations of services provided will always remain the top priority for the staff of Builder's Electric. In a field as competitive as electrical contracting, it's the courtesy, the honesty, and experience that has helped make Builder's Electric one of the true leaders in the business. □

# Twin Rivers Plumbing

**For 25 years Dick and Sandee, owners of Twin Rivers, have been able to deliver materials and manpower in a hurry.**

Founded in 1977 by Dick and Sandee Gerber, Twin Rivers Plumbing has grown to be the largest plumbing company in the Mid-Oregon area. Specializing in commercial and industrial plumbing, the family owned and operated company also does small remodeling projects as well as larger, high profile jobs in the area. Such projects and businesses as the Knight Law Center at the University of Oregon, Lane County Juvenile Justice Center, Chambers Media Center, Registered Guard, Eugene Library, Symantec, Autzen Stadium, and Sony Disc Manufacturing have all benefited from the fine workmanship that Twin Rivers Plumbing offers each of its clients.

This labor of love began in 1964 when the Gerbers were married. Having known each other since the ninth grade at Willamette High School, Dick Gerber worked as a plumber until deciding that he was ready to try his hand at running his own plumbing company. Utilizing Sandee as the business office's manager and with the help of several of the area's most experienced estimators, plumbers, design build team, and office staff, the Gerbers have managed to turn their dreams into a multi-million dollar business. The business has been so successful that it has afforded the Gerbers the opportunity to open a satellite office in Central Oregon where their daughter Shelley is the manager to handle even more of the business that it has incurred.

The Gerbers are quick to admit that without its staff of 75 people, none of this would be possible. By treating the employees with respect and recognizing their assets to the company as a whole, Twin Rivers Plumbing is able to select only the best employees to staff their company. The Gerbers share a special bond with their employees, sponsoring several activities to provide morale boosts throughout the year. From golf tournaments to company barbecues and weekend excursions, the staff at Twin Rivers Plumbing is treated like family because they are family. It is because of this attitude that Twin Rivers Plumbing has experienced a low turnover ratio over its decades of business with several of its employees remaining faithful to the Gerbers for 20 years and more.

This genuine kindness has spread from inside the business to the community at large, as Twin Rivers Plumbing has helped several projects and charities throughout the years. Organizations such as Scar Jasper Mountain, the Relief Nursery, and the American Red Cross have all benefited from the generosity of Twin Rivers Plumbing as the company believes that you get back from the community what you put into it.

With a deep pride in its workmanship, as well as respect for its employees, clients, fellow contractors, and community, Twin Rivers Plumbing has discovered the secrets of success and will continue to exercise them in the decades to come. □

**Twin rivers team 2002.**

PHOTO BY STEVE TERRILL

FIRE & EMS HEADQUARTERS
POLICE FIRE AND 911 TRAINING

# Chapter Twelve

# 12

## *Health Care & Education*



The health, education, and general well being of the community are exemplified by Eugene's fire and EMS headquarters, which serves as a training facility for police, fire, and 911 professionals. Photo by Charlene Sabini

# Spencer View Dental Park

With all the various businesses in the Eugene-Springfield area, one business has managed to bring more smiles to the faces of Lane County residents than any other.

Spencer View Dental Park was built in 1984 and the dentists began setting up office in 1985. With six general dentists and one orthodontist, Spencer View Dental Park is equipped to handle every dental need from teeth cleaning to teeth straightening to smile enhancement.

One of the original seven partners is Dr. George McCully. Deeply rooted in the Eugene area, Dr. McCully is a graduate of the University of Oregon Dental School (now Oregon Health and Sciences University). He sincerely believes that in both work and personal life you have to keep learning and evolving to have the opportunities to help others and make a difference in your community. Each year he attends over 200 hours of advanced training to keep abreast of the latest in dental care and technology. Although he considers himself a continual student, he demonstrates his commitment to serve by using every opportunity to teach and share what he learns. Always striving to improve, McCully carefully selected a staff who share his same values. They developed into such a special team that they have become a second family to him. Their shared commitment to quality and care is evident when you speak to their patients, who, although varied in ages, make one constant comment, "Everyone in Dr. McCully's office makes you feel like you are the most special patient they have." That coupled with his exceptional dentistry is what has made him successful.

McCully is devoted to his family, his wife Diane, daughter Sarah, 27, and son Sean, 24. His family's code, to serve others and improve oneself, appears to have been passed down through the generations. His family has been very active in Rotary Youth Exchange, which strives to promote good will and better friendships throughout the world. They have hosted countless youth from Sweden to South Africa. His daughter, Sarah, has participated in the program and brings back her experiences to share with others. His son, Sean, is currently working to become a physician. McCully says this level of caring and involvement started at his father's knee.

A vital member of the Eugene community, Dr. McCully has served as president of the Eugene Rotary Club, has been a member of the Eugene Chamber of Commerce, as well as a member of the Oregon Board of Dentistry. He has been active as a scoutmaster and as a coach. He has raised thousands of dollars for such organizations as the Lane County Auditorium Association that preceded our Hult Center, the YMCA, and countless other community organizations. He has a strong love of the outdoors, has served as a soccer referee and for over 25 years as a hill chief for the Ski Patrol. McCully delights in explaining his motivation. "My father always taught me, when you leave this world it should be a better place than the one you entered." Somehow, I believe he is meeting that goal.

McCully played a large part in the design of Spencer View Dental Park, when he joined Dr. Barry Beget, the founding partner, with the original vision of the park. Dr. Beget realized that to accomplish his goals of creating an esthetically pleasing and publicly inviting courtyard to host leading-edge dentistry, he would need to find some exceptional dentists who shared his vision. He found six partners and Spencer View Dental Park became a reality. The pride and dedication they put into achieving their goals for the complex is evident to the hundreds of locals who pass through the courtyard daily. The plantings around the complex were designed by world renowned landscape architect Dr. Ron Lovinger, a professor in the Department of Landscape Architecture at

One of the original seven partners is Dr. George McCully.

Another winning smile from Spencer View.

the University of Oregon. The plants reflect many of the species that are found in the Eugene area, keeping the park as natural as possible.

Dr. Beget has been working with his patients to design their perfect smiles for 25 years. He has created thousands of smiles, and it hasn't all been from braces. For 13 years, each week he has taken great joy in visiting and reading to the elderly, has been a consultant to the Cranio-Facial Defects and Rehabilitation Clinic, remains active in the Eugene Southtowne Rotary Club, and has served on five medical missions to third-world countries. He sponsors local athletic teams and donates time speaking at our schools. Beget truly believes in giving to our community and to others less fortunate. His staff proudly boasts that it is his ethics and caring that make him successful as both an orthodontist and as a leader.

Recently remarried to a "phenomenal woman," Beget is also the father of three "remarkable sons." (He says he's sure there is no bias in these statements, you just need to meet them.) Beget chose the field of orthodontics because he loves children and he is especially compassionate toward all the adults, who didn't have the opportunity when younger, that are turning to orthodontics now. He takes equal care to ensure that both children and adults are comfortable and relaxed while in his office. The office philosophy is to make a trip to the orthodontist as fun and pain-free as it can possibly be. His office of nine staff members is full of laughter and enthusiasm, and the good times prove to be infectious as the patients enjoy coming to his office just as much as the staff looks forward to welcoming them.

Many of his patients keep coming back, not only to visit what became their orthodontic family, but also to visit the courtyard they enjoyed regularly. Located only a few blocks from South Eugene High School and the University of Oregon, students of all ages are invited to use the courtyard as a meeting place, a lunch spot, or just a shortcut to their classes.

Dr. Beget and Nikki checking the progress of her smile.

Neighbors and friends enjoy the lush, serene courtyard at Spencer View.

EXQUISITE LANDSCAPING HAS ALWAYS BEEN AN ATTRACTION AT SPENCER VIEW.

"We're always getting positive comments from people about the appearance and atmosphere of the complex," says Dr. Jim Sweeney, another of the founding developers of the Dental Park.

A general dentist, Sweeney performs a wide range of procedures including veneers, bleaching, and implant restorations. His overall knowledge of the field of dentistry is reassuring to his patients in that he's able to handle nearly every dental problem that they may encounter.

Sweeney always excelled in science classes throughout school, and had a general idea that he would want to find an occupation that would focus on his interest in science. He decided on pursuing dentistry after going to an orthodontist

DR. SWEENEY AND "BEST FRIEND" IN THE FIELD.

as a child and enjoying the experience. After graduating from dental school in Portland, Sweeney spent a few years in the U.S. Army as a dentist before coming to Eugene to open a practice of his own. A few years later, he was offered the chance to be part of the Dental Park and took advantage of the opportunity.

A married father of one child, Dr. Sweeney enjoys spending time outdoors when he's not creating better smiles for his patients. An avid fan of bird hunting and fishing, Sweeney also enjoys racquetball and basketball. Having attended the University of Oregon prior to dental school, Sweeney has called Eugene home for over 40 years.

Throughout the years, Dr. Sweeney has helped thousands of patients through his ability to communicate with each of them, helping them understand what he is able to provide for them and listening to what their desires may be from him as their dental care provider. He is also a firm believer in the concept that the appearance of the Spencer View Dental Park is playing a large role in his success.

"I think the facility itself brings a reflection of the quality of service that patients can expect to receive when they come to us," Sweeney says. "Patients see the outside of the Park and witness how well the grounds are kept up and maintained. And when they see the quality that we maintain in the building and complex, they feel confident that they will receive the same attention to quality in their dental work."

Dr. John Robinson feels as strongly about the Spencer View Dental Park as his colleagues. "There are so many advantages to being a part of the Spencer View Dental Park," he says. "The proximity to the Y, the University, the high school, and the housing. Everyone knows where it is because it's in such a visible location."

Originally from Colorado, Robinson graduated from Washington University in St. Louis. After living all over the West and Midwest, he decided to settle down in Eugene and buy a dental practice. After a few years, he discovered that the Dental Park had an opening and he jumped at the chance to become a part of the dental dynasty.

As a health care provider and former president of the Dental Society, Robinson feels a great deal of responsibility to his patients to inform them of exactly what he's capable of doing for their smiles. This is especially true in severe cases where he has to explain the options to his patients. He makes a serious effort to stress the importance of the consequences to patients when they don't follow through with their dental treatments.

A husband and father of three children, Robinson cites his attitude as a key to his success. He believes in having fun at work and keeping a light, casual atmosphere at all times. His six staff members truly enjoy coming to work for him with many of them staying by his side for several years. Dr. Robinson values the communication he receives from his staff and is always available to listen to their concerns. As he says himself "Anybody who thinks they know it all is in trouble."

From the building to the courtyard to the doctors themselves, the dentists at Spencer View Dental Park are clearly in the business of creating smiles. They believe in providing and exercising "service above self," a saying that they've borrowed from the Rotary Club. And they manage to provide this service through laughter, faith, trust, and most importantly—making their patients feel better about their smiles and themselves when they leave the complex. □

**Quality family dentistry.**

**A beautiful smile created at the complex.**

# University of Oregon

Although it was the members of the Oregon Legislative Assembly who passed a bill in 1872 establishing a state university in Eugene, it was a grassroots effort by the community that kept alive the dream that would one day create the University of Oregon. In 2001, the UO marked its 125th anniversary as the premiere liberal arts and sciences research university in the state.

Money was scarce in the early years, so the local community of Eugene ambitiously agreed to supply the building if the legislature agreed in-kind to locate the university within its reach. "The Building" was planned to be larger and grander than any other building in town, so this determined community organized a door-to-door campaign to its 1,000 residents, producing contributions ranging from livestock to labor.

When the doors of Deady Hall opened officially for classes on October 16, 1876, with John Wesley Johnson serving as president, there were five faculty members and 177 students. By the turn of the century, the university's student population had grown to 456 students, and it was during these years that students formed the Associated Students of the University of Oregon (ASUO) and published the first issue of "Oregon Weekly," which in 1920 became the "Oregon Daily Emerald."

**All classrooms and facilities at the University of Oregon offer state-of-the-art technology for enhancing teaching and learning. In the Knight Library, (pictured) electronic resources provide students, faculty, and community members with access to a diverse range of materials, including contemporary and historical references to the sciences, humanities, and social sciences.**

A spirit of community activism—both locally and nationally—began to emerge in the early 1900s, and it has proven to be an important part of the university's history. During World War I, a British officer named Col. John Leader helped transform the University of Oregon into a military training ground to teach men how to march in formation and properly handle a rifle.

During World War II, it was not unusual to see students marching to class. Staff and students were dedicated to the war effort, sponsoring scrap drives, fundraisers, and blood drives through the American Red Cross. In 1944, the University of Oregon gained notoriety by raising more money for war bonds than any other college or university in the nation.

This activism continued throughout the 1960s, when sit-ins staged in Johnson Hall became the popular venue for students wishing to express themselves. And in 1994, the University of Oregon's record-breaking effort to register voters gained national attention and earned the campus the distinction of being one of the nation's ten "most activist campuses."

Through the decades, the university has diversified to serve the needs of not only its students but the public as well. Today the campus population has grown to approximately 19,000 students and nearly 5,000 faculty and staff members and student teaching assistants. The UO Alumni Association—organized in 1879 to "promote continued involvement after graduation" among the university's first five graduates—now serves more than 150,000 alumni and friends in 15 countries. □

**High-back wooden desks were characteristic of classrooms during the early years of the University of Oregon.**

# Lane Education Service District

If there is one entity in Lane County that is deeply rooted in shaping of the community past, present, and future, it would have to be the Lane Education Service District (ESD).

Established in the early 1800s when county superintendents were appointed to oversee each county's school districts, today Lane ESD helps schools meet the challenges of educating area children by providing leadership and educational support services in five general service areas. Those categories are Administrative Support Services, Technology/Learning Support Services, Curriculum/Teaching Support Services, Special Education Services, and Business Support Services.

Focusing on the 16 local school districts of Lane County, the Lane ESD offers all students an equal opportunity to receive a world class education-regardless of the size or wealth of the district in which they reside. Services and programs provided by the Lane ESD cover those which can prove to be too costly for some of the smaller districts to support or when a single location may have the need for a certain service, or there is a large demand for it, such as special education or technology services. By collaboration and coordination among the districts and other agencies, Lane ESD can moderate the costs for all which in turn conserves public funding of many services and programs, one of the biggest benefits of Lane ESD. With the entire Lane County supported by the ESD, this translates to over 3,000 educators and 50,000 students, along with other members of the community benefiting from the actions of this organization.

Funding for the cost effective services and programs offered by Lane ESD comes from a combination of grants, property taxes, state monies, and enterprise efforts. Every dollar that comes into the ESD gets maximized 16 fold, with the ESD obligated to provide a minimum of 90 percent of the money that it receives into resolution services to districts.

With the amount of money that the Lane ESD has been able to conserve, other programs have been able to benefit from those savings. For instance curriculum services created a planetarium several years ago which recently was cited to become a greater part of the community. While the planetarium was always open to the public, Lane County, the Fair Board, and the Lane ESD have come together to use the planetarium as a foundation to grow into a unique sophisticated science learning center, providing activities and experiences for Lane County children and placing the Lane ESD in the center of the community.

While in a constant responsive state of change, the Lane ESD is in a position of evaluating its services through the input of its customers and providing services that meet the greatest needs for the most people. While there are always variations on the primary programs each year, there is also dynamic, constant change amidst the various districts and the services provided. And at Lane ESD, the most important function is also the simplest—to continue to bring people together, to listen, and to respond. □

(TOP) LANE ESD CENTER FOR LANE COUNTY SCHOOL DISTRICT SERVICES.

(ABOVE) BRINGING PEOPLE TOGETHER TO SHARE SERVICES IS AT THE HEART OF LANE ESD.

# PeaceHealth

Outstretched hands form the foundation of a sculpture above the main entrance to Sacred Heart Medical Center.

In July 1936 four young nuns arrived in Eugene from Bellingham, Washington, to take over operations in a hospital whose elevator rarely worked and whose beds, one physician said, "would hardly qualify for a flophouse." They were from the Sisters of St. Joseph of Newark, already known in Washington and Alaska as excellent hospital administrators, who at the request of Eugene physicians had agreed to buy Eugene's ailing Pacific Christian Hospital for $50,000.

By the end of the century, Sacred Heart Medical Center had become one of the largest and most respected medical centers between Seattle and San Francisco and flagship for PeaceHealth Oregon Region, part of the health care ministry of what is now called the Sisters of St. Joseph of Peace. No longer limited to providing just hospital care, PeaceHealth now includes PeaceHealth Medical Group, Eugene's largest and oldest multi-specialty medical group. It also includes Cottage Grove Community Hospital and South Lane Medical Group in Cottage Grove, plus Oregon Medical Laboratories, a reference laboratory for hospitals and clinics in three Northwest states.

It's a story not only of the commitment and vision of the Sisters but of the generosity of a community, which has pitched in to support every major hospital expansion, from a six-story wing completed in 1941 to the $3.5 million Campaign for Cardiac and Vascular Care completed in 1998.

Campaigns of this kind have helped make Sacred Heart a regional referral center for much of western Oregon. The Oregon Heart Center, one of the nation's top-ranked cardiac care facilities, was the first Oregon hospital outside of Portland to offer open-heart surgery. The Oregon Rehabilitation Center is a model for its effective, multidisciplinary approach to getting everyone from stroke patients to those with spinal cord injuries back into life. More than 1,000 people have hip or knee replacement surgery at Sacred Heart every year. And every year hundreds of premature or otherwise struggling newborns are transferred to Sacred Heart from other area hospitals to be cared for in the Neonatal Intensive Care Unit.

But advanced medical technology is just one reason PeaceHealth has become a national model for health care. Its nurse midwifery birth center has been singled out by UNICEF for its exceptional support of breastfeeding mothers. Every diabetic patient at PeaceHealth Medical Group is enrolled in a comprehensive program of continuous evaluation and education to prevent, rather than simply treat, complications. Harp, piano, and other live music is used at Sacred Heart to help create a calming atmosphere in public areas, to help promote healing in patient care areas, and—at the end of life—help ease the physical and spiritual pain of the dying.

As the 21st century dawns, PeaceHealth is planning construction of a new medical center to meet the community's growing need. After 60 years of hands-on administration by the Sisters, PeaceHealth has moved into a new era of lay leadership. But the mission and values that guided those young nuns in 1936 continue to guide PeaceHealth today: a commitment to collaboration, stewardship, and social justice, and a respect for individual human dignity and worth. □

Pediatrician Deborah Fuerth, M.D., coaxes a smile from a young patient at PeaceHealth Medical Group's Clinic South.

# Northwest Christian College

Originally founded as a divinity school in 1895, Northwest Christian College today offers educational opportunities in the arts and sciences and selected professions in an environment that fosters Christian faith, self-understanding, and responsible citizenship. The College plays a central role in developing the region's community leaders and neighbors.

Northwest Christian College takes seriously its role as a partner in Oregon's higher education. Trustees, administrators, and faculty use a continual process of planning and evaluation to assess ways the College can lead in a dynamic educational environment. Because of its small size, the College is nimble and able to respond quickly to changes in the academic landscape. Dr. Joseph Cox, chancellor of the Oregon University System, praises the College's responsiveness, saying, "NCC is quite skillful at finding educational needs and filling them in very creative and complementary ways."

Two among several exemplify the College's responsiveness:

### Elementary education major

The University of Oregon's termination of much of its teacher education program created a vacuum in the community. NCC responded with an elementary education major and master's degree program in school counseling that meet vital needs in the community.

### Degree Completion Program in Management for Working Adults

NCC administrators and faculty carefully designed innovative programs to help working adults complete a bachelor's degree or an MBA. Nearly 200 students enroll in these programs each year, and an impressive 85 percent of them complete their degrees. Satellite programs are offered in Medford, Grants Pass, and Roseburg. Students are employed by many of the region's leading companies, including Sony, Hyundai, Weyerhaeuser, Sacred Heart Hospital, EWEB, as well as area police and fire departments.

While the curriculum has been broadened over the decades, its program to prepare church professionals remains a vital part of the curriculum. Several hundred NCC graduates serve congregations of many denominations across the nation and around the world.

Northwest Christian College's values-based academic programs are designed to prepare students for advanced learning at leading graduate schools, for a professional career, for community leadership, and for service. The College's curriculum strives to integrate faith and learning into every discipline with an emphasis on evaluative thinking and effective communication skills.

Every academic major at NCC requires a significant internship experience, so students are routinely involved in businesses, community service organizations, schools, and churches to develop practical understanding to complement their academic studies.

**Built in 1908, the Goodrich Administration Building includes classrooms and financial aid and administrative offices.**

To instill the value of giving, all students perform community service. The College has established programs to provide students with opportunities overseas, in large U.S. cities, and in the local community. Last year, students contributed more than 38,000 hours in Mexico, Romania, the Philippines, Portland, Los Angeles, and San Francisco as well as with local agencies such as Sacred Heart Hospital, the Salvation Army, Eugene Mission, Looking Glass, and many public schools.

Professors with PhD's teach most classes, never a teaching assistant. NCC courses foster personal interaction and spirited discussions. Professors are approachable and take a genuine interest in the success of students. They become mentors. This time-honored tradition of shaping and molding exceptional graduates and leaders will continue to thrive and flourish. □

**NCC's Kellenberger Library provides online catalogs, databases, and virtual world-wide access through Internet and interlibrary loans.**

# Orthopedic Healthcare Northwest P.C.

**Dr. Thomas K. Wuest of Orthopedic Healthcare Northwest is an orthopedic trauma surgeon who often cares for patients with complex fractures.**

Orthopedic Healthcare Northwest P.C. was formed in 1995 when two orthopedic groups with long-standing reputations for medical excellence merged—Orthopedic and Fracture Clinic of Eugene and McKenzie Orthopedic Group. The affiliation resulted from a belief that each practice would provide enhanced patient care by combining their resources and working together. Today, the organization serves the West Coast from facilities in Eugene and Springfield, specializing in the treatment of bone, joint, soft-tissue, and related disorders.

Everyone at Orthopedic Healthcare treasures living and working in the Willamette Valley. The area's scenic beauty and outstanding quality of life attracts experienced professionals from some of the best training programs in the country. With contributions from such highly talented people, Orthopedic Healthcare Northwest's future growth and success is ensured.

Comfortable in its role as a contributing member of the Eugene/Springfield health and business community, the 105 employees of Orthopedic Healthcare Northwest have treated thousands of patients, helping them to once again enjoy daily activities. The group shares a strong commitment to giving each patient the personal attention essential to the healing process.

**Dr. Nancy M. Lynch specializes in hand and microvascular surgery at Orthopedic Healthcare Northwest.**

Modern technology helps the physicians at Orthopedic Healthcare Northwest successfully treat many injuries and other conditions that were previously considered disabling. The group's professionals routinely care for athletes from area schools as well as professional athletes from around the world. In addition, Orthopedic Healthcare Northwest provides team physicians for the University of Oregon's athletics program. As sponsors of the Donald B. Slocum Foundation for Research and Education for Orthopedic and Sports Medicine, Orthopedic Healthcare Northwest's doctors stay actively involved in research and teaching.

A full complement of experts support the group's experienced orthopedists: a podiatrist, physician's assistants, registered nurses, registered radiology technologists, cast and brace technicians, certified medical assistants, certified first surgical assistants, and registered physical therapists.

Looking toward the future, Orthopedic Healthcare Northwest is developing a comprehensive Orthopedic Center to improve the delivery of orthopedic and sports medicine services to the community. Orthopedic Healthcare Northwest, its physicians, and its employees all share a dedication to providing the highest quality medical care and the utmost personal attention to each and every patient. □

PHOTO BY BRUCE BERG

8TH AVE
THE TIFFANY
WILLAMETTE

# Chapter Thirteen

# 13

## The Marketplace & Tourism



Built in 1913, the Tiffany Building is one of downtown Eugene's most discernable landmarks. The elegant old department store building was recently renovated to accommodate a number of businesses and apartments. Photo by Charlene Sabini

# Valley River Inn

Spacious, comfortable guestrooms and suites.

For nearly 30 years, the beauty and elegance of Eugene's Valley River Inn has charmed both visitors and locals with its blend of comfort and stylish grace, creating a unique stay for all who stroll through its front doors.

Built in 1973 by a prominent local timber family, Valley River Inn has stood proudly as the premier hotel in the area. The inn was originally constructed in order to give back to the community of Eugene a hotel that would compliment the city's charm.

Situated in the heart of Eugene and resting on the banks of the Willamette River, the Valley River Inn is truly a site to behold. Steeped in history, a timber motif runs throughout the hotel, from the large wooden beams to the antique seven-foot diameter saw blade hanging in the lobby. The chandeliers in the lobby, made from vintage mill parts, are breathtaking in their beauty and ingenuity. The ambiance in the Valley River Inn not only exudes class and sophistication, but also pays respect to the area and its ancestors. In addition, Valley River Inn showcases several pieces of fine art from the River Run Gallery throughout the hotel, which are rotated on a continuous basis. These works of art follow a predominantly Northwest theme. The manicured lawns and gardens found throughout the grounds of Valley River Inn offer a splendid first impression to all that visit the Inn.

Valley River Inn offers its customers a variety of activities and amenities in one of the most gorgeous settings in the city. Such luxuries as valet parking, Espresso carts, fresh juice bars, an indoor sauna and whirlpool, full-sized swimming pool and bicycle and helmet rentals with over 11 miles of cycling, and running paths just outside the doors await those who choose to stay at Valley River Inn. For those who prefer to get their exercise walking store to store, the Valley River Center, Eugene's largest shopping mall, is adjacent to the hotel.

With 257 oversized guestrooms, three ballrooms and over 15,000 square feet of fully equipped meeting rooms capable of accommodating up to 600 people, Valley River Inn is the natural choice for those companies and corporations seeking a luxurious stay that can fully accommodate their needs. The scenic river views combined with the natural lighting, outdoor decks, and courtyards can give any event from a private party to a corporate convention the perfect setting that is not only peaceful but comfortable for each of the attendees. The professional staff at Valley River Inn is trained to meet the customer's every need and take pride in making each visit an enjoyable stay that will keep customers coming back again and again. A full time concierge is available to hotel guests and is the only one of its kind in Eugene.

Annual Valley River Inn-vitational.

Valley River Inn is also home to one of Eugene's highest acclaimed restaurants, SweetWaters. Featuring the best in Pan Pacific Northwest cuisine, SweetWaters is renowned for its delicious Pacific seafoods, North American game, and fresh produce gathered locally. Tantalizing dishes such as flash seared Yellow Fin Tuna with Sonoma Foie Gras and Pomegranate Glace de Viande, and Bittersweet Chocolate Strawberry Rasputin have earned the restaurant a reputation as one of the most elite establishments in Eugene. Comprised of a number of the best chefs in the Northwest including Chefs Michael Thieme and Paul Martin, this inspired culinary team present menus with a focus on clean refined flavors and chic plate presentations. The restaurant has received recognition from nearly every regional publication in the area including Bon Appetit, NW Palate, and Simply Seafood. Serving breakfast, lunch, and dinner, SweetWaters is also home to one of the most scrumptious Sunday brunches in Eugene.

The SweetWaters Lounge offers guests and locals a chance to hear some of the best jazz in the Northwest in a relaxing and refreshing setting. During the summer months, the activities billow out onto the open-air veranda that is adjacent to the lounge, providing a fun atmosphere in a glorious environment.

As Valley River Inn was constructed with the community in mind, it is the community that benefits most from its operations. Contributions and donations are made to several local and national organizations including the Oregon Bach Festival, the United Way and the University of Oregon. In addition, each August the Valley River Inn-vitational golf tournament is held to help benefit the Ribbon of Promise, a local organization that nationally helps educate students and teachers on strategies to help in curbing school violence.

LUSH GARDENS AND RECREATIONAL ACTIVITIES ABOUND.

With a commitment to grow and improve to best suit its customers needs yet stay true to its traditions, Valley River Inn shall continue to flourish for many generations to come. □

THE PLACE FOR SPECIAL EVENTS IN EUGENE.

# Germyn's Cleaning & Maintenance Service, Inc.

"I knew if I was ever going to make any money, I'd have to start my own business," Fred Germyn began. Fred discovered early in his working career that if he was going to be successful in realizing the life he wanted for himself and his family that he was going to have to pursue a business of his own. Disappointed after being laid off from his regular job for the second time, he looked elsewhere. A neighbor needed some help cleaning a few accounts and what began as a part-time job became Fred Germyn's future.

The work was demanding and the hours not the best, working primarily in the evenings, often from 6 p.m. to 6 a.m. Fred could see down the road to a better life. His father's admonitions that he should always do his best and that no one was going to give him anything he didn't earn echoed in his ears as he drove through the dark to his next account.

Days off were few and far between and family life was strained as the Germyn's struggled to secure their future. The business grew, but it also took its losses with changes in the economy, employees which came and went, competition took its toll of accounts, and the need to create stability in an industry which traditionally has an extremely high rate of turnover taxed Fred's patience. Despite the trials, Fred continued to abide by his father's words and continually committed himself to quality service.

One of Fred's talents is being able to see down the road and this vision of the future kept the business moving forward. A few years later Jim McMillan, then a representative for a consulting firm, stopped by one day on a sales call. Fred didn't buy that day, but a few months later they met again and decided to build the future of Germyn's together.

With new strategies in place to help reduce the turnover rate a new culture was born. "Because Fred had done such an excellent job of building a quality company and reputation in his business, it was easy to come up with solid marketing and business building strategies," said Jim. "Fred Germyn's commitment to doing an outstanding job was evident from our first conversation. I knew immediately that Fred and I had a winning combination.

McMillan continues, "One of the first lessons I learned about our employees was that people in the janitorial trade feel under appreciated. Money was not the deciding factor for most of our folks—it was much more how they were appreciated."

This fact prompted the decision to create an environment of appreciation and Germyn's began recognizing their employees with awards for such things as outstanding work, customer service, and professionalism. The company wanted to give its employees a genuine forum where they felt comfortable voicing their concerns, suggestions, and appreciation. It took about six months for employees to realize that the company was sincere in wanting to hear their opinions. Since then the monthly meetings have taken on a life of their own, giving the employees an unusual opportunity to play an active role in the direction of the company.

Fred and Jim strongly believe that when people have the opportunity to improve themselves, they are able to put more of their unique talents into their work and private lives and that in turn creates a

**From left to right: Jim Colton, operations; Robert Atkinson, supervisor; Fred Germyn, owner; Jim McMillan, general manager; and Travis Germyn, residential carpet cleaning.**

TRAVIS GERMYN REPRESENTING GERMYN'S RESIDENTIAL CARPET CLEANING PROGRAM AT THE LANE COUNTY HOME SHOW.

more productive, enjoyable environment for everyone. It is this belief that prompted the discussion of reading materials at all of the company's meetings. "We believe that reading is a prerequisite for just about any endeavor and certainly a critical ingredient for success," Jim says with conviction.

In addition to the meetings, the company issues a monthly newsletter, the Germyn's News, to inform the employees, customers, and potential customers about developments and to share a wide range of ideas. "We feel that it is critical to peoples' well being to be informed so we try to communicate regularly and openly with our folks," says McMillan.

Germyn's unique relationship with its employees is evident from the very beginning. While the application for new hires covers the basics, Germyn's has added their own twist to the form by asking potential employees to do some soul searching on the application.

"We ask them where they want to go in life," Fred says. "We don't want people thinking that these are jobs that anybody that comes in off the street can get. That's demeaning to the employees."

"We want people that can think and who have some aspirations," Jim adds.

Another unique approach to the business finds the management admitting something that most managers would like to keep secret. At Germyn's, they fully understand that it's the employees which carry the everyday activities of the business. In return for their efforts, though Germyn's cannot afford to pay high wages because of the nature of the business, they can enlighten each of the employees' hearts, minds, and souls with knowledge, recognition, and self-esteem boosts.

At Germyn's the bottom line is not just exceptional cleaning services. It's providing an uplifting and stimulating working environment in which exceptional employees can do exceptional work and become exceptional members of the community. Which, in turn, keeps the American Dream alive for everyone. □

# King Estate

While Oregon is home to over 185 wineries, there are none quite like King Estate. This gorgeous 820-acre estate is set amongst the sprawling hills of Southwest Lane County and is resplendent with magnificent vineyards, orchards, a nursery, and a lush organic garden surrounding the grounds. Resting atop of the hill is the winery itself, a state-of-the-art majestic building crafted in the style of a grand European chateau. Its beauty is evident from miles away and is truly an illuminating spectacle both inside and out.

The winery came to fruition in a unique way. The president of the winery Ed King, III first came to Lorane in order to secure some hay for his horses. While picking up the hay, Ed took a look around the farm and realized what a wonderful setting it would be for grapevines, having recently planted his first vineyard and understanding the qualifications for a successful venture. After discussing it at length with his father Ed Jr., the Kings decided to embark on a life-altering journey with the planting of its initial vineyard in 1991 and the building of the 110,000-square-foot winery that took two years to complete.

Since its inception, King Estate's mission has remained the same—to produce varietal wines of consistently exceptional quality. While no small feat, this is accomplished through meticulous fruit selection, impeccable winemaking practices, and judicious blending of the ingredients to provide wine connoisseurs worldwide with an impeccable experience.

The wine production at King Estate centers around three varieties: Pinot Noir, Pinot Gris, and Chardonnay. Several world-renowned wine critics have rated the Pinot Noir and Pinot Gris as some of the best tasting wines available on the market today. Each of the varieties are crafted into three tiers, the King Estate Signature Collection which is produced annually, the King Estate Reserve Collection which have a more limited production, and the King Estate Domaine and Vineyard Collection which are traditional yet innovative, classic, and rare. In addition to the wines, King Estate has published two cookbooks, which illustrate the interplay of flavors between food and wine, giving connoisseurs of the brand the chance to perfect a series of gourmet dishes at home using the Pinot Noir and Pinot Gris wines. Tours of the winery are also offered where visitors have an opportunity to witness how the wines are made as well as taste samples and purchase souvenirs from the gift shop.

The people at King Estate are passionate about their product and proud of the heritage that they are creating. One taste of the exquisite wines is all it takes to fully understand the genuine enthusiasm being generated atop this peaceful setting in the Oregon hills.

For more information about King Estate, tours, tasting schedule, and directions, please call (800) 884-4441 or visit www.kingestate.com. □

PHOTO BY BRUCE BERG

# Enterprise Index

**Builder's Electric**
195 Madison
Eugene, Oregon 97402
Phone: 541-485-0922
Fax: 541-485-4055
www.builderselectric.com
*Page 117*

**Centennial Bank**
One Southwest Columbia Street, Suite 900
Portland, Oregon 97258
Phone: 503-973-5556
Fax: 503-973-5557
E-mail: bscott@centennialbank.com
www.centennialbank.com
*Page 110*

**Eugene Airport**
28855 Lockheed Drive
Eugene, Oregon 97402
Phone: 541-682-5430
Fax: 541-682-6838
www.eugeneairport.com
*Pages 100-101*

**The Eugene Area Chamber of Commerce**
1401 Willamette Street
Eugene, Oregon 97401
Phone: 541-484-1314
Fax: 541-484-4942
E-mail: info@eugenechamber.com
www.eugenechamber.com
*Pages 108-109*

**Germyn's Cleaning & Maintenance Service, Inc.**
PO Box 2514
2091 Roosevelt Boulevard
Eugene, Oregon 97402
Phone: 541-689-4077
Fax: 541-688-0201
E-mail: germyns@televar.com
*Pages 136-137*

**Giustina Family**
*Mailing:*
PO Box 989
Eugene, Oregon 97440
*Street:*
1991 West Second Avenue
Eugene, Oregon 97402
Phone: 541-345-2301
Fax: 541-345-2305
*Pages 102-103*

**Home Comfort Heating & Air Conditioning, Inc.**
706 Oscar Street
PO Box 24205 *(Mailing)*
Eugene, Oregon 97402
Phone: 541-345-2838
Fax: 541-302-3070
E-mail: jeffe@ehomecomfort.com
www.ehomecomfort.com
*Page 104*

**Inovec, Inc.**
115 Wallis Street
Eugene, Oregon 97402
Phone: 541-485-7127
Fax: 541-485-4672
E-mail: sales@inovec.com
www.inovec.com
*Pages 94-95*

**King Estate**
80854 Territorial Road
Eugene, Oregon 97405
Phone: 800-884-4441
Fax: 541-942-9867
E-mail: info@kingestate.com
www.kingestate.com
*Page 138*

**Lane Education Service District**
1200 Highway 99 North
Eugene, Oregon 97402
Phone: 541-461-8222
Fax: 541-461-8298
E-mail: cwiggins@lane.k12.or.us
www.lane.k12.or.us
*Page 127*

**McDonald Candy Co.**
2350 West Broadway
Eugene, Oregon 97402
Phone: 541-345-8421
Fax: 541-345-7146
*Page 90*

**McKay Investments Company, LLC**
2350 Oakmont Way, Suite 204
Eugene, Oregon 97401
Phone: 541-485-4711
Fax: 541-485-4714
E-mail: linda@oakwaycenter.com
www.oakwaycenter.com
*Page 116*

**Monaco Coach Corporation**
91320 Coburg Industrial Way
Coburg, Oregon 97408
Phone: 541-686-8011
Fax: 541-681-8899
www.monaco-online.com
*Page 91*

**Northwest Christian College**
828 East 11th Avenue
Eugene, Oregon 97401-3745
Phone: 541-343-1641
Fax: 541-343-9159
E-mail: pres@nwcc.edu
www.nwcc.edu
*Page 129*

**Orthopedic Healthcare Northwest P.C.**
*Eugene:*
1200 Hilyard, Suite 600
Eugene, Oregon 97401
Phone: 541-485-8111
Fax: 541-342-6379
*Springfield:*
1435 G Street
Springfield, Oregon 97477
Phone: 541-746-9018
Fax: 541-744-2830
*Page 130*

**PeaceHealth**
PO Box 1479
Eugene, Oregon 97440
Phone: 541-686-6868
Fax: 541-687-4986
E-mail: bterrett@peacehealth.org
www.peacehealth.org/willamette
*Page 128*

**PSC, Inc.**
959 Terry Street
Eugene, Oregon 97402
Phone: 541-683-5700
Fax: 541-345-7140
E-mail: info@pscnet.com
www.pscnet.com
*Page 97*

**Sony Disc Manufacturing**
123 International Way
Springfield, Oregon 97477
Phone: 541-988-8000
Fax: 541-988-8099
E-mail: websdm@disc.sony.com
www.sdm.sony.com
*Pages 88-89*

**Spencer View Dental Park**
622 East 22nd
Eugene, Oregon 97405
*Pages 122-125*

**St. Vincent de Paul Society of Lane County, Inc.**
P.O. Box 24608
705 South Seneca
Eugene, Oregon 97402
Phone: 541-687-5820
Fax: 541-683-9423
E-mail: svdp@svdplanecounty.org
www.svdplanecounty.org
*Pages 114-115*

**Symantec**
555 International Way
Springfield, Oregon 97477
Phone: 541-335-5000
Fax: 541-335-5020
www.symantec.com
*Page 96*

**Twin Rivers Plumbing**
1525 Irving Road
Eugene, Oregon 97402
Phone: 541-688-1444
Fax: 541-688-9272
E-mail: sandee@twinrp.com
www.twinrp.com
*Page 118*

**University of Oregon**
Eugene, Oregon 97403
Phone: 541-346-1000
www.uoregon.edu
*Page 126*

**Valley River Inn**
1000 Valley River Way
Eugene, Oregon 97401
Phone: 541-687-0123
Fax: 541-687-0289
E-mail: normh@valleyriverinn.com
www.valleyriverinn.com
*Pages 134-135*

# Patrons

*The Eugene Area Chamber of Commerce and Community Communications, Inc. would like to thank the following companies for their patronage:*

**Affolter West & Jones Architects Planners, AIA, P.C.**

•

**Castle Rock, Inc.**

•

**Dwyer Shlesinger & deVilleneuve Attorneys**

•

**Johnson & Sherton P.C. Land Use Attorneys**

•

**Mystic Chicken & More! Inc.**

•

**Rexius Forest By-Products, Inc.**

•

**Satre Associates, P.C.**

•

**Summit Benefit & Actuarial Services, Inc.**

# INDEX

## G



## H



## I



## J



## K



## M



## N



## O

## P



## R



## S



## T



## U



## V



## W



## Y